The Visually Impaired:
Curricular Access and Entitlement in Further Education

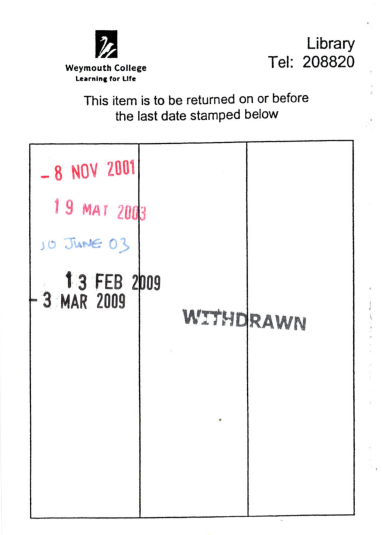

David Fulton Publishers Ltd
2 Barbon Close, London WC1N 3JX

First published in Great Britain by
David Fulton Publishers 1994

Note: The right of the authors to be identified as the authors of this work has
been asserted by them in accordance with the Copyright, Designs and Patents
Act 1988.

Copyright © David Fulton Publishers Ltd

British Library Cataloguing in Publication Data

A catalogue record for this book is available from the British Library

ISBN 1-85346-248-9

Designed by Almac Ltd., London

Typeset by RP Typesetters Ltd., Unit 13, 21 Wren Street, London

Printed in Great Britain by the Cromwell Press, Melksham

Contents

List of Abbreviations

ADC	Ability Development Centre
BESS	Basic Education and Skills Service
BTEC	Business and Technology Education Council
C&G	City and Guilds
CCTVs	Closed Circuit TV
DAS	Disablement Advisory Service
DEAs	Disability Employment Advisors
DES	Department of Education and Science
DFE	Department for Education
DL	Disability Leave
ERC	Employment Rehabilitation Centre
ERS	Employment Rehabilitation Services
FEFCs	Further Education Funding Councils
FEU	Further Education Unit
GNVQ	General National Vocational Qualification
GUI	Graphical User Interface
HELIOS	Handicapped People in the European Community Living Independently in an Open Society
HMI	Her Majesty's Inspectorate
HEFC	Higher Education Funding Council
ILO	International Labour Office
ILB	Industry Lead Bodies
LB	Lead Bodies
LEAs	Local Education Authorities
LVAs	Low Vision Aids
MSC	Manpower Service Commission
NAIMS	National Association of Non-Maintained Special Schools
NATSPEC	Association of National Specialist Colleges
NGO	Non-Governmental Organisation
NVQs	National Vocational Qualifications
OCR	Optical Character Recognition
PACTs	Placement Advice and Counselling Teams
PICKUP	Professional Industrial and Commercial Updating
QAC	Queen Alexandra College
RADR	Royal Association for Disability and Rehabilitation
RNIB	Royal National Institute for the Blind
RNID	Royal National Institute for the Deaf
RNC	Royal National College
RSA	Royal Society of Arts
SKILL	National Bureau for Handicapped Students
SNAC	Special Needs Advisory Committee
TEC	Training & Enterprise Council
TIDE	Technology Initiative for Disabled and Elderly People
TSSVI	Tertiary Service for Students with a Visual Impairment
TVEI	Technical Vocational Educational Initiative

FOREWORD

Sometimes described as a transitional stage, further education is very much more than this, offering students opportunities for study, practice and personal growth appropriate to their own levels of maturity. It may coincide with increased independence or with a return to learning to update skills. As a team of writers, the contributors to this book embody a positive and strongly based philosophy of providing and increasing equal opportunities in further education for all students. The students with whom they work and for whom they plan programs, support and provision have little or no sight. This is an inescapable fact, not to be confused with discrimination, but to be recognised as facing individual requirements realistically. Students may need adaptations in materials, in methods or in the use of technical equipment, they may require environmental modifications if they are to have realistic access to the curriculum. There are both well-tried and innovative solutions to such problems evidenced in the wide ranging contributions to the chapters in this book. In offering such solutions, the writers show perceptiveness and human qualities as well as technical expertise, and this results from their own experience in working with students in specialist colleges and in mainstream colleges offering support to students who are visually impaired. This is, in fact, a thoroughly practical book growing from a sound theoretical base.

However appropriate and well conceived courses in further education may be, they are of little help to visually-impaired students if they cannot take them up! The reader of this book is guided through the complex and changing aspects of student funding and support, and is alerted to the growing opportunities of interaction with other European countries. In this context it is interesting to note the number of highly developed and well established courses in the United Kingdom for students with a visual impairment. As the reader will discover in this text it is equally evident that access to the curriculum and entitlement to further education for visually-impaired students is an ongoing challenge.

Clearly from the contributions here, it is a challenge that is being actively and often successfully addressed.

Elizabeth K Chapman, OBE, MEd, BA, Dip.CTB
Hon Senior Research Fellow, University of Birmingham

INTRODUCTION

Access and Entitlement in Further Education

David Etheridge and Heather Mason

The chapters that make up this book are not primarily about disability or visual impairment. What they do address is the right of all people to have further education and training made available in ways that meet their needs, regardless of gender, race, age and ability. This book examines their entitlement to this education and some of the ways in which it can be made accessible. The issues raised are relevant to all people entering further education and training; what this book does is to look at specific ways in which they apply to people with an impairment of sight.

Entitlement has been defined as 'a right to participate in certain learning experiences in addition to working towards particular outcomes' (FEU 1990). An impairment of sight does not remove that right. Neither does it mean that people who are visually impaired have a special entitlement that differs from any adult returning to education or a sixteen-year-old making the transition to college from school. Entitlement applies to all just as practical access to provision must take into account the needs of the individual whatever the reasons for those individual needs.

An entitlement curriculum has been defined as one which provides for learner-centredness that takes into account the wishes of the individual. It is a curriculum that is based on equality of opportunity and experience and one which stresses maximised accessibility so that no artificial barriers are placed in the way of access, either curricular or physical. It stresses the need for optimised progression of all learners to achieve their personal targets and the importance of guidance and counselling in order to support this realisation of potential (FEU 1990). The entitlement curriculum also requires flexibility on the part of colleges in making their provision so that individuals are not excluded for reasons that are not of their own choosing (FEU 1990). Most importantly, however, it is a curriculum that recognises the discrete needs of the individual at the same time as recognising the right of that individual to be equal. A student with a visual impairment is entitled to access not because of that physical impairment but because s/he is a person in her/his own right. As Oliver has observed, we must 'allow for choice and control in service provision within a universalist infrastructure' where consumers have social rights to these services (1989). A visual impairment is not a special need nor a disability but rather constitutes the right of an individual to appropriate access.

The need to widen access to learning has been increasingly recognised as an imperative in further education and training. This recognition has been partly effected by the economic demand for an adaptable and flexible work force and has led to a series of national initiatives in education and training which have attempted to improve access to learning, training, retraining and qualifications. Legislation has attempted to persuade providers to become more responsive to client need however that is defined, and radical curriculum change through the introduction of a new framework for qualifications has meant that further education is now in a state of flux that presents real opportunities of greater entitlement and improved access. However, the potential has to be recognised and then realised. What the contributions to this book do is to point to ways in which this equality of opportunity is being (or might be) realised in colleges.

It has been suggested that discussions of entitlement have led to the emergence of three dimensions which should be taken into account in planning and implementing policy. Policy formulation and service delivery on a national level is perhaps the most important of these, since without a recognition of entitlement on a national level service provision is likely to continue to be determined by the chance of geographical location and local provision. Gordon Dryden in chapter one of this collection examines the single most important statement of and influence on policy to appear in relation to further education – the 1992 Further and Higher Education Act. The Act is significant in the changes in funding of further education and training that it creates which in turn affect entitlement to appropriate provision. However, the precise effects of this legislation are still unclear. Although it is likely to have an advantageous long-term impact on improved facilities for all students with disabilities, much will still depend upon interpretation of duties and the use of discretionary powers. The 1992 Act has created the potential for a co-ordination of services which is so sorely needed. The same is also true of the new structure for rehabilitation services which enables access to further education and training for people experiencing a new impairment or deterioration of vision. As Brian Hewitt points out in chapter two, recent government initiatives can lead to a more client-centred and more accessible rehabilitation service. However, unless this is properly funded and properly implemented the new service will fail to meet the needs of the clients it is intended to serve. Until that is realised effective entitlement will be determined by the colleges themselves in their provision of services and their use of the opportunities that are available to them.

David Etheridge, in his survey of transition from school to further education (chapter three), suggests that although there are a number of statutory agencies that can and do contribute to the provision for visually-impaired students their failure to co-ordinate their services means that the practical and immediate solution must lie with schools and colleges in providing an infrastructure that recognises the implications of entitlement. Many examples of good practice already exist in relation to this second perspective of entitlement, the local provision of services, and one of these is examined by Paul Lynch's survey of the support services available in Sheffield (chapter four). Another is addressed by Mary Bennett in chapter five in relation to the technical updating and re-training services provided by a specialist college of further education for the visually impaired.

Eligibility through policy and provision is vital if entitlement is to be achieved. However, the third perspective in discussing entitlement, the modes of learning to which everyone is entitled, also needs to be addressed. Again the opportunity to do so is available through recent initiatives such as the NVQ framework. Pauline Jeffrey demonstrates in chapter six how the increasing emphasis on competence is in fact an invitation to equality of opportunity and a vehicle for access to the curriculum in further education and training. Assessment is a vital part of this new framework and also of programme design and service support. However, it is important that full and effective assessment of the individual is available. It has not always been possible to provide this due to the inappropriateness of much standardised assessment for people with visual impairments. Bernadette Caffrey in chapter seven looks at ways in which access to full assessment can be provided through the adaptation of common assessment procedures for individual use. Appropriate programme content is also vital if learners are to have access to the full curriculum; Maggie Rowe in chapter eight and Steve McCall in chapter nine address two important aspects of the programmes that can create greater access for adult learners in further education: counselling, braille and other communication skills.

The recognition of individual needs and the provision of programmes that allow the individuals to achieve their potential is surely the aim of further education whether at a local, national or supra-national level. As Terry Gould stresses in chapter ten, opportunities exist for colleges to use national and supra-national initiatives to create local entitlement for visually-impaired students through appropriate access, which can then be used in a circular way to contribute to and modify the formulation of national policy. What is important is that provision for visually-impaired students in further education and training should not be seen as a separate development which is discrete to a small client group. As the Further Education Unit has suggested, colleges should overtly recognise and facilitate access for all members of the community, thus enabling them to fulfil their potential through a fully available range of broad, relevant and balanced educational opportunities. Colleges should, offer a curriculum that is delivered in ways which maximise flexibility and responsiveness to individual needs, and that enables individuals to achieve the highest level of competence of which they are capable (FEU 1991). This volume is an illustration of the ways in which individual needs can be met, not as a response to visual impairment but as a response to individual entitlement and the questions of access that are part of that entitlement. As Stokely Carmichael said of equality 'No person can be healthy, complete and mature if he must deny a part of himself' (1968). It is vital that a recognition of visual impairment is also a recognition of entitlement to equality of opportunity and the issues of access that raises.

References

Carmichael, S. and Hamilton, C.V. (1968) *Black Power* (London: Cape).

Further Education Unit (1989) *Towards a framework for curriculum entitlement* (London: FEU).

Further Education Unit (1990) *Flexible Colleges: Part 2–A Planning Handbook* (London: FEU).

Oliver, M. 'Disability and Dependency: A Creation of Industrial

Societies' in Barton, L. (ed) (1989) *Disability and Dependency* (Lewes: Falmer).

CHAPTER ONE

Implications of the 1992 Further and Higher Education Act

Gordon Dryden

Various brief outlines of the Further and Higher Education Act are available, of which one of the best is from the Department For Education (DFE) itself. It was printed in the July 1992 edition of *Educare*, the journal of SKILL, the national bureau for students with disabilities. Rather than simply reiterate the basic factual information available in that journal I shall try to draw out the significance of the Act for visually-impaired students, but to convey the full implications of the Act it is first necessary to consider how it passed through Parliament. This is because of the temptation to regard legislation as a framework which, apart from some clarification on detail in the courts, is a clear and permanent guide to the rights and duties of respective parties; in the case of this Act funding councils, local education authorities, educational institutions, students and the DFE. The amount of clarification needed for different pieces of legislation varies, but in the case of an education act which changes fundamental aspects of the education service, the need for regulations, guidance – and no doubt, in the long run, interpretations decided in court – is enormous. This is especially the case where it follows so quickly upon an earlier act that the notion of a stable legislative framework is undermined. For that reason the Act is perhaps best regarded as a stage in the development of further and higher education services which will be subject to modification over the next few years and is likely to be susceptible to continued lobbying.

The Further and Higher Education Act alters the funding responsibility for further education by taking it away from local government and placing it with funding councils, one for England and one for Wales. Higher education funding will be the responsibility of separate Higher Education Funding Councils for England and Wales, combining the roles of the Universities Funding

Council and the Polytechnics and Colleges Funding Council. The changes in funding responsibility were so fundamental that yet another new act was needed; this presented an opportunity for organisations representing students with disabilities and learning difficulties to seek to clarify the duty of the funding body to meet the needs of the students they represented. These organisations were concerned that the Act should establish the best practice by local government as the norm, rather than the worst practice. When the white paper was published these organisations, which included the Royal Association for Disability and Rehabilitation, the Royal National Institute for the Blind, the Royal National Institute for the Deaf, the London Boroughs Disability Resources Team, Rathbone and the Spastics Society, formed a campaign core group chaired by SKILL. They produced a charter which was used as the basis of a sustained lobbying campaign.

Unusually, the Bill went through Parliament with many of its clauses attracting negligible debate; 80% of debate concentrated on the first eleven clauses and the main single focus of debate was provision for students with special educational needs. An official at the DFE, closely involved in steering the legislation through Parliament, admitted that the Government had not been prepared for this imbalance and lobbying by the campaign core group was able to take the initiative on briefings during the debate. The result of this activity was that a number of changes were reluctantly conceded by the Government. This left the Act with some lack of clarity as the Government tried to minimise concessions whilst being seen to accommodate the disability lobby. Many of the detailed implications of the legislation are currently being worked out by the Further Education Funding Councils for England and Wales (FEFCs) and by the Higher Education Funding Councils for England and Wales (HEFCs). The DFE has issued guidance to local education authorities (LEAs) and discussions are under way between FEFCs and LEAs to clarify their respective responsibilities. With so much of the detail needed for implementation still to be worked out as guidance it is difficult to establish precisely what a visually-impaired student has a right to expect. Nevertheless, it is possible to identify changes that were made between the first draft of the Bill and the version that was finally enacted which give some indication of gains that have been made. It is also possible to identify concessions which represent limited explicit improvement but rather greater implicit improvement.

Main duties

General duty to have regard to the requirements of students with a disability or learning difficulty

Section 4 of the Act requires the Council to have regard to the requirements of persons having learning difficulties in carrying out their duties under sections 2 & 3. This is similar to Part II, section 120, Clause 10 of the 1988 Education Reform Act which requires a local education authority to have regard to the requirements of persons over compulsory school age who have a learning difficulty. Section 4 of the 1992 Act goes further in requiring a Council to secure provision, and accommodation if appropriate, for students who are not yet 25 years of age if suitable provision is not available within the maintained sector. This particular change was made after the committee stage in the House of Lords and predictably, being a major change made in a hurry, its implications are very unclear except in relation to a small number of students who are secured provision outside of the sector. It is clear that a student with a visual impairment who has not attained the age of 25 will, if suitable provision is not available within the maintained sector, be secured provision outside of that sector. It is equally clear that the FEFC will pay appropriate funds to an independent college where the provision is secured. The term 'secured' would otherwise be inappropriate. Where a residential placement is appropriate and agreed by the Council, the Council will also fund the independent provider for residential costs. A gap left by the legislation is the status of students with a learning difficulty, aged from 19 to 25, who are studying within the maintained sector. Some disability organisations have argued that such students could be charged for access to courses within the maintained sector and the FEFCs have not confirmed that such students would have a right to free provision. That, however, is the assumption of the DFE official who was responsible for co-ordinating work on the Act and was the view of several members of the House of Lords who were involved in the lobbying. It does seem extraordinary to suggest that a student can start a course in a residential college, all costs met, and then transfer to a college near home in the second year to face a bill for tuition fees. That is a matter which requires clarification. A further cause of doubt is the matter of who decides whether or not provision in the maintained sector is satisfactory. There is ample evidence of local authorities refusing out-county placements to visually-impaired students and insisting that they attend inadequate or even totally unsupported local provision.

Duty to seek expert advice

During debate in the House of Lords the Government would not concede that there should be a member appointed to each funding council with knowledge or experience of students with disabilities or learning difficulties. It was agreed instead by Lord Cavendish, on behalf of the Government, that funding councils would be required to seek expert advice as a condition of funding. Officials at the DFE and the funding councils have, in keeping with this condition, liaised with the campaign core group and the FEFC for England has also made it clear that it will be appointing its own quality assessment staff who will include appropriate specialists in provision for students with disabilities. Expertise at this level will not have a direct impact on service delivery at college level but it does ensure that issues concerning students with disabilities, particularly funding issues, will be informed by an awareness of students with disabilities at a strategic level. It will also enable the funding councils to better understand the implications of assessments which recommend placement outside of the maintained sector.

Duty to fund provision

Schedule 2 of the Act lists the kind of provision for which the FEFCs are responsible and in the first version of the Bill was concerned solely with courses leading to recognised qualifications, higher education access or basic education. In the course of parliamentary debate it was agreed that this should be extended to include courses in independent living and communication skills for students with learning difficulties where they lead on to any of the other courses listed in Schedule 2.

Duty to provide transport – Schedule 8

At present LEAs have a duty to have regard to the requirements of persons above compulsory school age for provision and for transport. Schedule 8 does reiterate that an LEA should make such arrangements for transport as it considers necessary and that this should be free. In theory this applies to adults with a disability or learning difficulty but provision of transport is only obligatory for students of the same age as pupils in schools maintained by the authority, in effect up to the age of nineteen. In practice provision of transport is very patchy and for students over nineteen years of age with a disability only a minority of local authorities provide transport. It is possible that the focus on students with disabilities achieved by amendments to the Bill will make it more difficult for local authorities to ignore their discretionary powers with regard to transport. For students who reach their nineteenth birthday during the academic year some LEAs might feel tempted to interpret their duty to provide transport in the same way that they interpret the funding of students in further education at present, cutting off funds on a student's nineteenth birthday. In discussion with officials at the DFE, however, it was pointed out by them that an age limit for a duty to provide a service implies that the service should be continued to the end of the academic year in which the birthday falls. In the case of transport this would be the academic year in which a student's nineteenth birthday falls.

Assessment

The need for a binding assessment was a central issue for the RNIB within the campaign core group. During the debate in Parliament no arguments were offered against the need for assessment. Lord Cavendish made it clear in debate that a funding council could not carry out its duty to have regard to the requirements of students with disabilities without first finding out what those requirements were. There was even some enthusiasm expressed at ministerial meetings for developing a procedure along the lines of the individual Action Plans being developed by the Employment Department. Nevertheless, the Government insisted that the issue would be best dealt with by guidance and nothing was put on the face of the Act. The question of assessment has been referred by the FEFC for England to the Further Education Unit as a project which is expected to make recommendations on assessment procedure in time for the September 1993 intake of students and the 1994-95 budget cycle. In the meantime the FEFCs will continue to use whatever method happens to be in use by LEAs.

This is the least satisfactory aspect of the Act since it is not possible to have regard to the requirements of students with disabilities and learning difficulties without a proper process of assessment. It places a particular responsibility on individuals working with visually-impaired students to ensure that assessments are carried out – but at present such assessments have no formal status. There needs to be an assessment procedure which is given sufficient weight to prevent FEFCs or LEAs opting for cheap alternatives which are inappropriate to the needs of students. For example, how is the FEFC to be satisfied that suitable provision is available within the maintained sector in carrying out its duty under section 4 of the Act? There is a danger that all but a handful of multiple-handicapped students will be obliged to attend local colleges which offer inadequate support because they are very much cheaper than specialist providers outside the maintained sector. Unless the assessment procedure is independent of FEFC and binding there is a danger that decisions will not be made with the student's needs as the priority. Unfortunately, the track record of a number of LEAs is such that there is every reason to feel that only an independent and binding assessment procedure will meet the needs of students.

Part-time students

There was an attempt by the campaign core group to use the Act as an opportunity to establish an entitlement for part-time students to receive the same benefits as full-time students where they are part-time as a direct consequence of their condition. This was directed at payment of fees and transport for students in further education and, for students in higher education, mandatory awards and the disabled student allowance. The Act offers no gains for part-time students, a serious matter for visually-impaired students since the majority study part-time out of necessity rather than choice. This arises from the extra time and effort needed for visually-impaired students to access information but is particularly significant where a student has additional conditions which together make full-time education impossible. This is certainly the case with some students with diabetic retinopathy who also undergo dialysis. There are several hundred visually-impaired students in further education in England and Wales with additional handicaps for whom part-time education is the only option. They are currently reduced to the level of second class citizens by the government's refusal to extend to them the financial benefits enjoyed by students who are able to attend full-time. This is one area where the lack of a sense of permanence in the legislative framework is something that RNIB and other organisations will exploit to lobby for further gains.

Differential funding

The delivery of appropriate services at institutional level which take account of the needs of students with disabilities will be a matter for the institutions themselves to determine. Their decisions are susceptible, however, to pressure from funding councils which have the power to set conditions to funding. An issue which is not yet clear is the intention of funding councils with regard to differential weighting or additional funding that might encourage institutions to provide suitable facilities for visually-impaired students. Historically, local education authorities have tended to use differential weightings, ostensibly to offset extra costs incurred by meeting the needs of particular student groups but sometimes at a level (three times the normal unit of resource, for example), which indicates a very positive policy steer. It is unlikely that any funding council will offer such a generous weighting but the FE funding councils are more likely than the HE funding councils to offer differential weighting. This arises from their position of picking up the role of local education authorities where differential weighting for special educational needs has been the norm within schemes of delegation drawn up in accordance with the 1988 Education Act. The HE funding councils, however, will be combining the roles of the Polytechnics and Colleges Funding Council, which was willing to explicitly target funding, and the Universities Funding Council which preferred to hand over a block grant and leave everything to the institutions to decide. It might be some years before the HE funding councils develop a differential funding formula weighted to encourage provision for visually-impaired students. It is, nevertheless, important to recognise that the requirement outlined earlier that funding councils must take expert advice on disability issues is likely to have a significant long-term impact on funding arrangements which might well lead to improved facilities for all students with disabilities.

Discretionary powers of local authorities

As the FEFCs, LEAs and colleges implement the Act there are grounds for concern over the use of discretionary powers. In the past, discretionary powers of LEAs have been applied with enormous variation between local authorities, with the level of service enjoyed by students varying from good to non-existent. The Act places a duty to have regard to the needs of students with learning difficulties and provides powers to meet this general duty. This could include the provision of support staff, discretionary awards to pay fees and maintenance and the provision of transport beyond the age of nineteen. Some LEAs have exercised these powers in the past with sensitivity and even generosity but others have been extraordinarily mean-spirited, in effect, refusing to use discretionary powers at all. Discretionary powers imply that the provision involved is not part of a fundamental right. It is a case of being desirable but not essential. A visually-impaired adult whose educational progress has been delayed by the impairment, or who requires further education because of a deteriorating condition, might well have a different view as to whether provision is essential or not. In these circumstances it may make sense to monitor the way in which an LEA uses its discretionary powers. If the Act requires LEAs to have regard to the needs of adults with learning difficulties there should be some evidence of students with disabilities receiving support appropriate to their disabilities. If there is no such evidence it is difficult to argue that the LEA is meeting its legal obligations. A recent example of an LEA failing to have regard to the requirements of a student, which would be equally relevant under the new legislation, involved the LEA refusing to pay the fees of a partially-sighted student because she had failed to achieve four GCSE passes at grade C, an entry requirement established by the LEA as appropriate for a BTEC course. RNIB argued that determining academic suitability is the responsibility of the college and that the LEA was failing to have regard to this student's needs by applying criteria which failed to recognise the impact of her visual impairment on the time needed to access information and produce work. To expect her to have done more subjects at GCSE level was unrealistic. The LEA conceded the point and agreed to provide funding. The principle that there must be evidence of differences between the treatment of students with learning difficulties and disabilities and the treatment of the rest of the student population, which are appropriate to the disability, is likely to be the most fruitful way of monitoring the use of discretionary powers by LEAs but it is very unsatisfactory that students should need intervention by a voluntary organisation to secure their rights.

14

Monitoring institutions

Assuming that FEFCs and LEAs carry out their duties, funding colleges to meet the needs of visually-impaired students and monitoring their performance, what should we realistically expect to find by way of extended opportunities and additional support?

The first point that the institutions themselves must consider is where to begin. Where there is a track record in further education it will frequently be of discrete provision of special needs classes. In higher education there is likely to be very limited experience of working with visually-impaired students. Nevertheless there has been a substantial increase in the number of visually-impaired students in further and higher education. Approximately 1550 were known to RNIB in 1992, but this includes a majority studying on a part-time basis. There is also evidence of a widespread willingness within institutions to develop suitable support facilities, but this trend is limited by a tendency by colleges and universities to favour a 'centres of excellence' model of development. This has been consistently opposed by RNIB on the grounds that it unreasonably restricts the range of choice available to visually-impaired students in comparison with their fully sighted peers and on the practical grounds that it needs little by way of additional resources to meet the needs of any student with only a visual impairment. Clearly there are further considerations to be taken into account where a multiply-handicapped student needs support.

There is a practical problem of implementing the Act where staff awareness and expertise is low in addition to a lack of support technology. There will need to be a period of time during which the understanding of visual impairment by teaching and support staff needs building up. However the level of training required is very basic and, given the lead in time to the implementation of the Act, there is no reason why any college or university should be unable to offer adequate support to a visually-impaired student from 1 April 1993. Where there is legitimate scope for an institution to seek some delay is in making particular curriculum areas accessible. There are subject areas which need a great deal of work to make them properly accessible to visually-impaired students. Accountancy and some areas of mathematics have been notably difficult in the past. There is also some legitimacy in an institution wanting to get its support procedures working properly before widening curriculum options but, provided that the visual impairment is a single handicap, there is no reason why all institutions should not be able to cope by seeking appropriate advice to work out a development plan for introducing access technology, a capacity for training students in the use of that technology and a programme of staff development.

It has to be emphasised that the process of assessing what a student needs and what is a reasonable provision of support by a college or university is a matter of interpretation. Where the cost of providing technology and support is modest there is every reason to suppose that institutions will be expected to meet student needs. The difficulties are likely to be acute where a student has additional handicaps and may wish to have a residential placement outside of the maintained sector where specialist support is highly developed. The assessment procedure may well identify needs accurately and make an appropriate recommendation as to the kind of provision and support that should be made available. There are still likely to be a number of cases where a student will be obliged to attend a local college which has only basic support facilities that do not adequately meet the student's needs because of the lack of accepted criteria for levels of support appropriate to particular conditions.

This dependence on interpretation and the use of discretionary powers is obviously going to be a source of difficulty in relation to individual cases. It is useful in these circumstances to have shared guidelines with the funding councils and this is a likely future development. The kind of features that would be taken to indicate an institution's willingness to help the funding councils meet their duty under the Act in relation to visually impaired students might be:

- information available in large print, in braille and on tape;
- publicity that states a commitment to meeting the needs of students with disabilities;
- a handbook for students with disabilities;
- a policy document on meeting the needs of students with disabilities;
- an opportunity for students to visit a campus prior to the start of term to familiarise themselves with the layout;
- a development plan indicating: the levels of support staff, the use of access technology; training for students in the use of the technology; career planning and guidance; a staff development programme for both teaching and non-teaching staff.

16

Conclusion

It cannot be over-emphasised that the 1992 Further and Higher Education Act lacks clarity, requires a great deal of supplementary guidance and will be open to continuing pressure for amendment because of its failure to address issues that are going to be a source of constant embarrassment to its authors and those who work within it. The circumstances of part-time students is perhaps the most glaring issue of this kind. The result is that a commentary of the kind made on the 1944 Education Act which remained relevant for decades is no longer appropriate. The emphasis in relation to the 1992 Act, certainly for anyone concerned with provision for visually impaired students, is on regulations and guidance and options for seeking further amendment. It has to be conceded that an unpromising Bill has been developed into an Act which, perhaps because of its faults, has still managed to open up some improved opportunities for visually-impaired students.

References

DES (1988) *Education Reform Act* (HMSO).
DFE (1992) 'Further and Higher Education Act 1992: Education for people with learning difficulties', *Educare* 43, 3-4.

CHAPTER TWO

Adult Rehabilitation for Visually-Impaired People

Brian Hewitt

This chapter examines the philosophy and curriculum involved in rehabilitation for the visually impaired. It then goes on to address the issues raised by the regionalisation of rehabilitation and possible strategies that might be adopted for future provision.

Definitions

In many parts of the world the term 'rehabilitation' embraces the total range of services for disabled people from infancy to old age. In Britain, however, it is accepted that a person passes through a process of rehabilitation following an accident, illness or some other trauma which has rendered them physically, sensorially or psychologically impaired in a manner which adversely affects their quality of life either socially, vocationally, or both.

Rehabilitation programmes are of necessity client-based and therefore vary widely in nature, content and duration, although components of each client's programme can be fairly accurately predicted in consequence of a period of initial assessment prior to the commencement of that programme.

Ideally, rehabilitation programmes should be of an holistic nature incorporating concurrently or sequentially all of the elements appropriate to meet a client's needs. Unfortunately, however, for a combination of political and funding reasons this is frequently not the case, despite the fact that British legislation and the philosophies and statements of the International Labour Office positively promote and certainly do not exclude the holistic programme.

Origins and definitions in Britain

The 1944 Disabled Persons' (Employment) Act defines employment rehabilitation as follows:

> The provision of 'Industrial Rehabilitation Courses' for disabled persons was stated to be to 'render them fit for undertaking employment, or work on their own account or for making use of a vocational training course and to offer such other incidental facilities as may appear to the Minister to be requisite for enabling persons attending an industrial rehabilitation course to obtain the full benefit'.

Whilst the main thrust of the above is towards rehabilitation components of an industrial/employment orientation, it also appears to recognise the need for aspects of social rehabilitation to be encompassed within a client's programme where this is of real benefit to that client.

The 1948 National Assistance Act (Section 29, part 3), as amended by the Local Government Act 1972, empowers a local authority to make arrangements for the welfare of 'Persons who are blind, deaf, or dumb and other persons who are permanently and substantially handicapped by illness, injury or congenital deformity.' In 1974 (LAC 13/74) the Secretary of State directed that the groups to be covered by the arrangements should also include the partially sighted and that there was a mandatory requirement on local authorities to make arrangements to provide:

- a social work service and such advice and support as may be needed for people living in their own homes or elsewhere;
- facilities for social rehabilitation and adjustment to disability including assistance in overcoming limitations of mobility or communication;
- facilities for occupational, social, cultural and recreational activities;
- arrangements for the keeping of registers of persons to whom Section 29 applies.

Regrettably, however, what now frequently happens in Britain is that the Employment Service regards its funding responsibility as extending only to rehabilitation components which are clearly vocational, on the grounds that social rehabilitation is the statutory responsibility of local authorities. The latter, for a combination of reasons, seem unable to meet this obligation.

ILO (International Labour Office) definitions:

It is worthy of note that the ILO guidelines are implemented throughout most of Europe. Under the heading 'Vocational Rehabilitation and The Employment of the Disabled' the International Labour Office (ILO) quotes the following definitions relating to adult rehabilitation:

32 Co-ordination of rehabilitation services

The working together of public and private agencies to ensure that the disabled persons receive all the necessary educational, medical, vocational and social services in a thorough, smooth manner. This co-ordination implies that referrals to services will be made when needed so as to avoid any unnecessary or harmful delays. To assure effective co-ordination, it is often essential that one professional person, or agency organise and follow through a rehabilitation plan with each disabled person.

54 Social rehabilitation

That part of the rehabilitation process aimed at the integration or re-integration of a disabled person into society by helping him to adjust to the demands of family, community and occupation, while reducing any economic and social burdens that may require the entire rehabilitation process. (WHO)
[Social rehabilitation is considered a vital part of all rehabilitation processes (e.g. medical, educational and vocational). It also refers to a disabled person's own experience and efforts to overcome various environmental barriers or limitations, these include legal, attitudinal (prejudice), physical (architectural), etc., barriers or limitations.]

59 Vocational rehabilitation centre

A facility which may provide some or all of the following assistance to help disabled persons to gain or recover their work capacity:
1. help and guidance on social problems which may impede resettlement
2. physical reconditioning
3. medical, psychological, social and vocational assessment of capacity to function in or perform particular types of work
4. improvement in morale and self-confidence
5. vocational preparation and training
6. placement in suitable employment. A sheltered workshop or

home work programme may be attached to a vocational rehabilitation centre (re: employment rehabilitation centre, industrial rehabilitation unit, rehabilitation centre or facility, work preparation centre, work evaluation centre).

From the foregoing it will be appreciated that the true nature of rehabilitation as understood by the International Labour Office and in Britain is a process following trauma, aimed at restoring normality and quality of life to the sufferer.

Components of adult assessment and rehabilitation

Having defined the meaning of rehabilitation we move on to identify its main components and the process necessary to identify the appropriate composition and delivery of a 'client-centred' rehabilitation programme. In this context the term 'client-centred' is crucially important as being indicative of the fact that unlike most forms of education, further education and vocational training, the participant does not have to abide by pre-set curricula aimed at achieving an academic or vocational qualification, but that the curricula/rehabilitation programme has to be drawn up and implemented in a manner to meet the specific situation and needs of each individual client without the need for all clients to aim at a near identical outcome.

Component parts of rehabilitation are mentioned randomly in the ILO definitions at the beginning of this chapter but in summary they comprise the following, either in total or in any combination as appropriate to each individual client.

Initial assessment

This will be necessary to determine need with regard to medical matters, physical considerations, sensory impairments, psychological factors relating particularly to self-perception and motivation, social and family issues, personal finance, independence and day-to-day living matters. In addition, it will establish whether the client has aspiration or potential to retain or acquire paid employment. Particularly with regard to the latter, additional factors come into play, such as an assessment of the client's communication skills, numeracy skills, manual dexterity, educational and employment history and employment aspirations.

The very broad spectrum of assessment dictates that the total process will, of necessity, be carried out by a team of multi-disciplinary assessors working in an inter-disciplinary manner under the leadership of a co-ordinator whose job it is to draw together the findings of all team members in order to compile an assessment report and an action plan outlining how assessed needs and strengths of each client can be addressed in a subsequent programme of rehabilitation.

The assessment team will need to comprise – or, more likely, have access to – medical personnel, clinical, educational and occupational psychologists, benefits rights officers and social workers, teachers, and low vision therapists. Ideally, these professionals should also have experience of working with clients suffering specific impairments and disabilities, i.e. mental illness, hearing impairment, visual impairment etc., as each impairment has special assessment and rehabilitation implications.

Rehabilitation programme and process

The action plan arising out of initial assessment will have recommended the nature of the rehabilitation programme appropriate to a client and will probably have given an indication as to where, how and when the programme should be provided and roughly how long it might take to achieve its objectives. However, all of these issues must be regarded as variables according to the availability of human, material and financial resources and also in the light of the continued assessment and monitoring which necessarily form part of the rehabilitation programme. Continued assessment will, in particular, have a bearing on the content and duration of a client's programme which may therefore be shorter or longer than initially anticipated .

An early decision must be made as to whether the client's rehabilitation programme will be implemented incrementally by various providers in different places at different times, or whether it will be provided holistically by one provider with the ability and resources to provide or facilitate all aspects of the client's action plan.

Ideally, the philosophy of 'client-centred' provision dictates that both options should be equally available to all clients, but in reality the timing and nature of service provision are governed by national and local politics, funding issues and geographical factors such as the proximity of facilities to a client's home. In reality therefore, the client has very little influence as to the nature, location and duration of their rehabilitation.

In Britain both social and employment rehabilitation provision arose out of acts of parliament during the 1940s, i.e. the 1944 Education Act and the National Assistance Act of 1948. The former required central government to fund employment rehabilitation whilst the latter placed a statutory responsibility on local government to fund and provide social rehabilitation. Unfortunately, this designation of two types of rehabilitation and different funding responsibilities has increasingly become a major obstacle to providing holistic rehabilitation programmes to visually-impaired clients. Most clients require social and employment-related components in their programme; in the interests of efficiency, and also their convenience and motivation they require all elements to be delivered simultaneously, but because central and local government will not fund what each sees as the other's responsibility, and because no arrangements exist for dual or multiple-funding, delay and confusion frequently arise to the detriment of the client.

Visual impairment provision

All of the foregoing refers to the structure of rehabilitation provision generally and represents the framework within which specialist assessment and rehabilitation provision for visually-impaired people operates. What has not been brought out, but must be mentioned in passing, is that a certain amount of rehabilitation provision is funded and operated by health authorities and hospitals, but that this does not apply to visual impairment in any major way.

For adults with visual impairment, social rehabilitation is the statutory responsibility of local authority social services departments. Some of these employ specialist staff of their own whilst others buy in the services they need or can afford from voluntary agencies for the blind which are registered charities and as such frequently subsidise the cost of providing services or provide some services on a voluntary basis. Most social rehabilitation of this type is provided to clients on a domiciliary basis but is frequently extremely limited in availability and scope, due to inadequate financial and specialist human resources. In consequence many blind people do not receive the social rehabilitation they need, as indicated in a survey 'Blind and Partially Sighted Adults in Britain' Volume 1, 1991 published by RNIB in 1991.

Between 1940 and 1991, employment rehabilitation for visually impaired people has been provided in two distinctly different ways. Firstly, it has been provided as a non-specialist service within the government's network of 26 employment rehabilitation centres throughout Britain and, secondly, through Britain's only specialist assessment and employment rehabilitation centres (ERCs) at Manor House Torquay, opened by RNIB in 1941, and Alwyn House, Ceres, in Fife, opened by the Edinburgh Society for the Blind in 1951 but taken over by RNIB in 1987. Both of these centres are still fully operational and working to capacity. However, the statutory responsibility for funding employment rehabilitation rests with central government, whose responsibilities are managed through the Employment Service which is part of the Department of Employment.

Major differences between the two types of provision were that the government centres traditionally made no special provision for visually-impaired clients and that 24 of the 26 were non-residential and did not therefore offer any residential or care support services. They were therefore only a viable option to those whose rehabilitation needs for visual impairment reasons were comparatively minor.

By comparison, the two specialist centres were equipped and staffed specifically to meet the needs of visually-impaired clients and have concentrated on developing appropriate resources, criteria and programmes to meet the needs of adults with a major visual impairment, including those with no sight and also those with an additional hearing impairment.

Manor House and Alwyn House employ the types of professional staff mentioned previously, but in most instances such staff also have additional professional qualifications and/or significant experience in appropriate areas of visual impairment which provides a service very much on a par to specialist educational provision.

Without going into detail, suffice to say that the curriculum of employment-related provision at both specialist centres mirrors that of the government ERCs and is consistent with areas described under 'Initial assessment' above. However, apart from each area being covered within its own context, it is additionally dealt with in a manner which relates subject criteria to the visual status of each client, involving the use of sight enhancement and/or sight substitution methods as appropriate. The centres thus operate a dual curriculum simultaneously with the mainstream curriculum and the visual impairment curriculum. With regard to the latter, there are subjects such as mobility and braille which are unique to visual impairment and thus are both subject and visual impairment curricula.

A strength of the government ERCs was their nationwide spread and their potential closer proximity to where visually-impaired people live, thus affording comparative ease of access between home and centre. On the other hand, because there are only two specialist centres, the majority of clients attend on a residential basis and therefore have to leave home for between two and three months, the prospect of which can throw up problems or prevent attendance altogether. However, the very positive side of residential attendance is constantly mentioned by clients who speak in glowing terms of the hugely beneficial effect of peer group support and of the tremendous amount of informal rehabilitation and stimulation which goes on around the clock in the lounges, dining room, and during on- and off-campus recreational and social activities. Also, there are numerous instances where it can be an advantage for a newly visually-impaired person to be away from a shocked and over-protective family, which tends to produce an unhelpful and negative environment for at least part of their rehabilitation process, albeit that the family must, of necessity become part of that process at the appropriate time.

Regardless of whether a client embarks on a programme of employment rehabilitation at a government ERC or one of the RNIB specialist centres they should, ideally, have followed a programme designed and conducted in a manner to meet their specific needs. The chances of this being so are clearly increased by attendance at a centre which specialises in visual impairment.

Obviously, programme content will vary from client to client with components being taken from a menu which includes specific or general counselling, vocational guidance and work sampling, job-seeking skills, mobility, orientation and independent living skills, confidence building through leisure and community activity, and advice and instruction in low vision enhancement and/or vision substitution techniques.

Officially, initial assessment and subsequent programmes of employment rehabilitation are separate entities, the latter being the implementation of an action plan arising out of assessment. In reality, however, employment and/or social rehabilitation programmes are a form of continued assessment by virtue of the fact that each client's programme performance is constantly monitored in conjunction with the client so that the programme can be modified to take account of special needs and circumstances. For instance, a client may embark on a very broadly-based programme and as strengths and weaknesses are identified the programme can be modified to cut out subjects for which the client shows little or no aptitude so as to devote more time to subjects for which the client has a need and interest or some aptitude.

The rehabilitation process combines the programme components mentioned above and involves the delivery of these via a partner-type arrangement between each client and each member of staff throughout the programme. In these circumstances staff with specialist knowledge and experience of rehabilitation and visual impairment most often deliver the most appropriate type of service to visually-impaired clients.

The role of the rehabilitation manager or co-ordinator of any service or centre is to monitor the overall performance of staff and clients and, on completion of each client's programme, agree with the client the content of a report of programme performance and outcomes and an action plan identifying short to medium-term aims and objectives and how best to pursue them. The client should then be provided with a copy of the report and action plan, with copies being provided to potential sponsoring agencies, organisations or individuals relevant to implementation of the action plan. Ideally, the service or centre which produces the action plan should also establish a mechanism for follow-up in order to monitor the extent to which it is being implemented or the extent to which action needs to be taken to assist implementation.

The future

Under current government philosophy and planning all of its 26 employment and rehabilitation centres will close and be replaced by nine ADCs (Ability Development Centres) during the early 1990s as part of a policy to establish a regionally operated employment service incorporating assessment, rehabilitation, training, counselling and placement. The precise nature and role of ADCs has still to be defined, but it is likely that they will provide a small amount of rehabilitation direct to clients and that they will be involved in employment-related research and development projects, including staff development. The new service will bring together into

PACTs (Placement, Advice and Counselling Teams) staff who previously worked in each of the separate disciplines of Department of Employment services.

PACTs will provide some services direct to clients and will also have budgets and a role to buy whatever specialist services they consider appropriate from private contractors offering rehabilitation, training, counselling, or whatever is required and available.

The philosophy behind this major change in service provision is one of making the maximum amount of provision available as close as possible to where a client lives in order to increase accessibility, reduce personal inconvenience and hardship and increase relevance of service provision to the client's local environment. The government also anticipates that this type of regional service will be less expensive than the traditional service and that it will therefore be able to pay for an increased number of clients to benefit.

The philosophy of taking service as close as is practicable to the client, rather than always requiring the client to come to the service seems sound, but what has to be tested and closely monitored is whether uniform service criteria for all regions can be agreed, implemented and monitored for quality and outcomes.

There is a danger that, particularly during the early years of the new service, quality of service delivery through a diversity of new contractors with little or no experience in rehabilitation and related services will be variable, ranging from good to poor, thus adding considerable hardship and suffering to clients – many of whom by virtue of needing rehabilitation, are already at a very low ebb.

Bearing in mind the very special needs of newly visually-impaired clients, it is clear that central government and organisations concerned with specialist services for visually-impaired people, must liaise and work co-operatively in order to ensure that the nature, quality, and availability of employment rehabilitation services are guaranteed. The level of government funding of regional services and PACTs must also be set and maintained at a level to pay for the additional costs necessarily incurred by making appropriate provision to meet the needs of visually impaired clients.

RNIB and other agencies for visually-impaired people are not opposed to the developing new service in principle, in fact many of its features are accepted as philosophically sound and will be welcomed if satisfactory implementation and operation can be achieved, paying due regard to the concerns previously expressed.

It is likely that for the immediate future the RNIB centres at

Manor House and Alwyn House will maintain their established pattern of provision whilst simultaneously entering into a more regional role involving the introduction of additional services relating to campus and outreach activity in employment training, support of students and staff in regional further and higher education, social services, health services and with others as opportunity arises.

Summary

The ILO definitions at the opening of this chapter promote the simultaneous delivery of all components of a client's rehabilitation programme regardless of whether various elements are categorised as social or employment-related. In Britain today, however, this is extremely difficult as funding of these two elements is the statutory responsibility of two separate agencies and there is no established mechanism between them for total funding, joint funding or co-ordination of any client's programme. This is an issue which seemingly must be resolved as a matter of great importance if clients are not to be offered no service, inadequate service, or fragmented service, none of which constitutes rehabilitation as defined at the outset.

Safeguards

An optimistic view of the foregoing is that, if funded and implemented appropriately, the government's intentions for the future of rehabilitation services could herald a new service which is both client-centred and more accessible to a greater number of clients than its forerunner. The converse, however, is that if under-funded, funded in an incoherent manner, or poorly implemented, the new service will substantially fail to meet the vitally important rehabilitation needs of thousands of people needing help with overcoming the effects of illness, accident or some other trauma.

Issues such as adequate and coherent funding mechanisms, nationally agreed rehabilitation criteria for regional programmes, staff qualification, delivery performance of regional providers, monitoring of rehabilitation outcomes, and an advocacy/consultancy service for clients are all of such importance as the new service develops that they cannot be left to chance. They need to be monitored and guided by a mechanism which has the authority to highlight and counter shortcomings.

The above could almost certainly be achieved in a number of ways, but one possibility might be the establishment of a 'rehabilitation services inspectorate' operating in similar fashion to the long-established schools and colleges inspectorate so as to monitor the performance and outcomes of rehabilitation providers. Such a team might be provided and funded either by central government or, alternatively, members of the inspectorate might be employed by a major voluntary/private agency under contract to the government. In any event, the two prime roles of such an inspectorate must be, first, to ensure that the nature and availability of rehabilitation is truly appropriate to the needs of potential and actual clients and second, to ensure that people in need of assessment and rehabilitation services receive maximum support and advice with regard to obtaining the range of services they need in the most appropriate manner.

The rehabilitation inspectorate might need to function at two levels, one involving rehabilitation consultants/co-ordinators whose job it is to be primarily caseworkers and client advocates and another level of officers acting as inspectors to maintain an overview of the entire rehabilitation scene.

The need for monitoring of developments in the field of rehabilitation for the remainder of the twentieth century is crucial in the interests of all prospective rehabilitees. For visually impaired people in particular it is of paramount importance, bearing in mind the highly specialised needs of this tiny section of the population, needs which can so easily be under-regarded if a multiplicity of inexperienced and non-specialist providers enter the field of employment and social rehabilitation.

CHAPTER THREE

The Transition to Further Education: Provisional Perspectives

David Etheridge

At the age of sixteen or very soon after young visually-impaired people, in common with their sighted peers, are required to make a transition from childhood to adulthood. This may involve a locational change from one educational institution to another. It will certainly involve a curricular change from programmes justified by the National Curriculum to those which are determined more by employment and/or higher education. It is likely that it will involve a change from educationally-based programmes to those which are informed and justified by training needs and expectations. Above all the change will involve a break with the child-centred ethos of school and entry to an environment which is intended to be, and is informed by, preparation for full adult status and the expectations that go with it.

This transition happens at a stage in a young person's development when biochemical change and the shift from expectations of dependency to responsibility mean that the young person feels least able to cope personally with that process. Difficulties created by social perceptions of sensory impairment will not help. Nor will having to make a commitment to decisions that are likely to have a significant future effect at a time when society and the economy are themselves in a process of flux. Many make the transition successfully. However, with such a combination of destabilising factors facing the young visually-impaired person, to say that the transition process is challenging would be to grossly understate the situation. What the young person will find in further education is likely to be wholly different to what they will have experienced before. The size and complexity of the buildings will vary according to the college, but they are likely to be larger than anything in the secondary sector. This, together with greater numbers of people, will create a bewildering, seemingly hostile and impersonal environment even after the most careful mobility and orientation training. Colleges appear large and chaotic places where the breadth of the curriculum will rival the buildings in its handicapping complexity. Choice of courses ranges from the familiarly academic to a profusion of professional and training qualifications. This wide curricular choice has become more complex with the modularisation of courses and the changes that are being introduced as a result of the recent training initiatives. NVQs and GNVQs have added a new structure to a system which is already complicated by the multifarious awards from BTEC, C&GLI, RSA and the professional training bodies, whilst other courses are in the process of mutating to new forms.

Greater choice and freedom can itself be a threatening thing when it comes without preparation; constant flux in the tertiary sector militates against stability and security. The fact that further education is non-compulsory, with a quite different adult, libertarian and client-based contract between the parties assumed to be in operation, can act as both a threat and an opportunity for those new to it. Indeed, it can often lead to an indistinct dividing line between liberty and licence which can itself lead to intense personal insecurity after the formal certainty of school. The process of change created by recent legislation is having its effect on the status of colleges and the conditions of service of staff; these changes will indirectly affect the visually-impaired student by determining the level and expertise of service that is available to her/him and thereby affecting course availability. Dealing with transition has rarely been a high priority in further education and the needs of visually-impaired students in this process have received even less attention in an era when numbers have become all-important. In some cases this has been a conscious policy based on the argument that further education should be a fresh start for all, without ideas and assumptions being carried on from secondary schooling. As HMI have observed, few colleges considered it worthwhile to ask for information about new students, a serious situation when many LEAs have left this responsibility to the colleges themselves (DES 1991)

Bureaucracy has compounded the situation rather than alleviating it. In educational terms an adolescent who has been helped by a statement of individual educational need loses this protection when s/he leaves the protection of the school. Indeed, as the HMI report

24/91/NS observed, few LEAs 'have addressed the management of the process of transition for young people with special educational needs, that is, of planning the change from one phase of education to another. Discontinuity of provision is evident where this has not occurred.' (DES 1991). In some LEAs the sensory support services have included the tertiary as well as the primary and secondary sectors of education in their responsibilities; others have left this sector to service support organised by the colleges themselves. This again can vary from inclusion as part of the broader general support for moderate and severe learning difficulties to very specialised sensory support. Individuals with visual impairments have a wide variety of needs which will vary from situation to situation. Transition is one of these in which the nature of the needs change as special needs and handicap are redefined.

Administrative decisions rather than disabilities may decide whether an individual who is blind is defined as such and thereby receives extra assistance. Even where this support exists the effect may be more disabling than supportive. McGinty and Fish have listed up to 35 categories of professionals including education, social services, health authorities, voluntary services and employers who may make contributions to the transition process for a young visually-impaired person (1992). Many of these contributors to transition work in isolation from each other. Young people and their families face uncertain choices, a lack of coherent and positive information about their entitlement to education, support and training as they leave school. HMI found that few LEAs had a policy which addressed transition; in many cases LEAs assumed that this could be safely left to individual colleges and schools . They explained this situation as partly a result of financial constraints and the low priority given to special needs after the age of sixteen (DES 1991). However, McGinty and Fish have been less kind, stating that they feel that the situation is not always due to a lack of resources but rather a result of 'limited understanding and inadequate planning for transition' (1992).

Young visually-impaired people making the change from secondary to further education after sixteen will be coming to the process with a variety of personal, emotional, social and physical strengths and weaknesses and experiencing these changes in a variety of environments. However, whether the transition is a harrowing experience or a well-supported change, the student will inevitably experience a cycle of reactions and feelings which is usually described as having seven phases (Hopson, B. and Adams, J. D., 1976). These phases represent a cyclical process which involves experiencing the disruption, gradually acknowledging, testing and understanding that reality and finally incorporating appropriate changes into behaviour. Phase one is often described as immobilisation and is characterised by a sense of being overwhelmed. In the context of this transition from secondary school to further education it will often show itself in a feeling that the amount of work that is required has increased immeasurably. The difficulties in accessing information or presenting work resulting from problems of sight appear to become an impassable obstacle that produces an inability to make plans or project into the learning process and its completion. Many young visually-impaired people at this stage will require confidence boosting and help with making work plans. They need a well-structured environment. Indeed, part of the ability to function as an equal in sighted society is founded on the ability to organise one's environment in such a way as to fulfil the needs imposed by that particular sensory impairment. The intensity of the experience will vary according to the individuals concerned and the environments in which they find themselves but if the problem is not addressed the experience is likely to be such an overwhelmingly negative one that they are likely to give up. Indeed, the drop-out rate at this stage, either from college or from one course to a less demanding one, is often very high.

Phase two is characterised by recognition of the problem and represents a positive move in that it is a way of coping with the mammoth tasks that are believed to exist. Young people often trivialise the changes they are experiencing or the demands that are being made on them. Most teachers in further education will recognise this stage in the sudden and dramatic decrease in work generated by a student and the seemingly nonchalant way in which s/he will approach the demands made. However, this phase rarely lasts for long and leads into a third phase of depression. Depression is the result of beginning to recognise fully the change that has occurred. Frustration will often result in deciding how to deal with the new requirements that are being made of the individual and will lead into the fourth of the phases, that of accepting reality. The attachment to old ways of doing things will begin to lessen at this stage. Students will often begin to take a greater interest in their new college and will begin to socialise more, albeit at varying levels of involvement.

This social involvement will help to provide a bridge to phase five in which the individual will start to test the situation by trying out and experimenting with new behaviours. However, the increased expectations that characterise this phase may sometimes result in outwardly negative reactions of anger, frustration and irritability with people or situations. They will often be very active and very demanding of those around them, trying out new ways of coping with their physical environment and becoming often passionately aroused by stimuli or ideas. This is followed by a cognitive search for meanings and recognition of the changes that have been experienced. Indeed, this sixth phase of the transition is often one from which it is difficult to break free. Tutors and counsellors in further education will recognise this phase as being one of frequent contact with a student characterised by long, involved and often circular discussions. Given a successful completion of this internalising process the result will be the final phase of transition, of full acceptance and conceptualisation of the change.

The challenges facing a young visually-impaired person making the transition to further education are legion and should not be underestimated. In addressing these challenges it is vital first of all to recognise that transition is an important process through which all adolescents must pass at, or soon after, the age of sixteen. As has been suggested, in the emotional transition that a student passes through the most important response should be a positive one of understanding and help rather than the often negative response of requiring the individual to immediately accept the normalising process of educational institutions. It is vital that all those people who have contact with young people experiencing transition, whether they be lecturers, trainers, tutors, heads of departments or team and section leaders, should be aware of the pressures that are brought to bear on these young people by what seems an everyday experience. As McGinty and Fish have observed, for any young person to move successfully from one part of the system to another 'requires careful preparation, support and guidance' (1992). This process can only start once the needs have been recognised and until this is achieved transition will continue to take its toll of the talents possessed by young people.

Once it has been recognised that a serious problem exists then something can be done to address it. Many authors have emphasised the responsibility of government agencies in this. HMI observed in their survey that practice was best where LEAs offered guidance to institutions on transition from school to further education. They suggested that a number of strategies might be considered as appropriate to meet local need. One LEA had produced a detailed policy document on transition arrangements spanning schools and further education whilst another, finding this process too cumbersome, preferred to use cross-phase advisers to ensure that the issues were addressed. One particularly progressive LEA had addressed this provision as part of its service of learning support, had included it in the continuum of entitlement and access for students with special needs and had therefore allocated an additional level of support (DES 1991). These developments are positive in that by recognising the issues at an LEA level they are effectively raising awareness across the educational sector. However, if transition is to be effective it must be seen as more than part of special needs provision. Discrete provision is likely to marginalise what should be available for all. Indeed, as has been the case in much of the provision for visually-impaired people, it will be more effective if it is addressed in the context of all the population rather than made it a special case. The emphasis on LEAs in the present insecure climate when their roles are being reconsidered, also begs the question as to how much longer this leadership will be possible. Certainly the question of resource allocation from a rapidly dwindling account is likely to an eloquent argument against such an approach.

LEAs are not, however, the only agencies who have responsibility for, and the resources to make a contribution to, the smooth transition of these young people. Strategic inter-agency planning at a senior management level has been identified as an important starting point for a co-ordinated and effective provision. Support for the process should be part of the brief of inspectors, advisers, educational psychologists, peripatetic teachers, social workers and all the other professionals identified by McGinty and Fish as having an important contribution to make to the well-being of visually-impaired young people (1992). The NAIMS/NATSPEC report of April 1991 also recommended that transition should be the subject of a published code of practice from the relevant authorities which would then guide the actions of those authorities and provide an additional element of accountability. What is most important, however, is a recognition that they are contributing to an individual transition plan and not a separate plan for each sector.

Another area where central planning would be appropriate is in the provision, as recommended by Hinds to NAIMS/NATSPEC, of a

Transition Pack. This could take the form of an information pack to be distributed to the young people and their families and carers, possibly via the specialist careers officer, or the head teacher of a maintained special school or unit. The obvious time for this to be used in the first instance would be at the review of children who are subject to statements which occurs when they reach the age of thirteen. Indeed, such a review would be useful to inform the present and future needs of all visually-impaired children. Information on LEA, local and national provision should also be included. Questions of anticipated outcome, future lifestyle and accommodation could also be addressed within this; it would be designed to be used on a multi-agency basis, in conjunction with the young person and their parents/carers. Similar information could also be used at leavers' conferences and careers conventions within an interview situation. The precise nature of this would need to be explored separately, having different implications for both schools and colleges. However, it is vital that such a pack should contain information about the options that are available at sixteen, names and addresses of people who would be able to provide more information and the level of support that will be made available to undertake the options, since this may vary with the college chosen. It is important that specialist options are also considered, even though they may be expensive and out of county. Visits to appropriate specialist colleges should be made available so that the choice made is an informed one. In turn these colleges should be encouraged to contribute to the Transition Pack or its equivalent.

Another function more appropriately provided by LEAs and other authorities at a local and regional level is awareness raising about the needs of young people experiencing transition to further education and training in strategies that might be adopted to help them successfully undertake the process. Such training might be made available to a number of different client groups. Parents and governors of schools and colleges should be made aware of the needs of these young people and the strategies that they might adopt to help them. The same is true of professionals working with these visually-impaired people in schools, colleges and in the social services. Indeed, so little has been done to address this need that the field is a very open one. Colleges and schools should address these training needs themselves and use the resources that are available to them to prioritise transition as an area in need of support.

In 1991 HMI made the point very strongly that there was a

pressing need at all levels for more carefully planned support to ensure a smooth transition to the next phase of education and training. The potential exists where there are effective LEA management procedures and joint school and college curricular planning: 'If these arrangements are to be carried through, further progress needs to be made on developing more flexible styles or provision and on providing a range of learning support which can enhance achievement within a broad and balanced curriculum' (DES 1991). The curriculum is an important area which needs to be addressed if successful transition is to be facilitated. Smooth transition is more likely to occur where there are bridging courses in colleges which accredit prior learning and where there is assessment leading to the provision of a range of individual learning support strategies. The potential vehicle for this is already in place in the form of the structure and requirements of courses which have been influenced by the National Council for Vocational Qualifications and the Lead Bodies which inform it. Unfortunately these new ideas are still only influential in the area of training and accreditation of prior learning. Assessment of the individual and the rights of the learner as a partner are still sadly lacking in the academic and the pre-NVQ/ curricula. Individual action plans, informed by the needs of a student in transition, are an important extension of present curricular developments.

In bridging the transitionary phase between secondary and further education the most common curricular vehicle has been the TVEI. Not only has a set of common modules helped to give continuity to the education of young people between the ages of fourteen and eighteen but the initiative has also encouraged institutional arrangements and communication which might not otherwise have taken place. TVEI also illustrates the importance of a common core curriculum which provides for a progressive updating of the skills needed to support the education and training of young people. Indeed, this need has been influential in creating other link courses that have helped to create structures for transition. These programmes should include modularisation of courses which enables integrated programmes to be delivered in both schools and colleges. Link programmes have been used to extend and complement the existing school curriculum and in some cases ease resourcing problems by utilising those of the local college of further education (DES 1991). They are often used as part of the elective element in the school curriculum although this can lead to a devaluing of the courses by students and a consequent lack of commitment.

The development of link courses has been pioneered in the special educational needs sector, particularly in the area of learning difficulties; this needs to be developed more by mainstream and special schools and units for the visually impaired using the possibilities provided by COMPACT arrangements and courses like the BTEC first awards or even GCSE. Certification is important if the link course is to have credibility. The formal importance of the course should also be demonstrated through sufficient allocation of funds and time for liaison and curriculum meetings. Senior management involvement also means that it is likely that the course will be fully supported and will be implemented. Regular meetings of headteachers and managers involved in the courses will help to raise the profile of the scheme and provide an effective forum for implementation. In one authority a college special needs co-ordinator was able to gain access to LEA policy and planning meetings and in another a head was seconded for a year as a special needs co-ordinator in further education (DES 1991).

SKILL, in their survey of transition arrangements, have shown that a true partnership between college and school is central to the successful operation of link courses. But links need to be seen by schools as more than just an introduction to college life. They need to take into account furthering the curriculum of the school (Corbett 1990). Duplication of provision should be avoided and college attendance should be a specific part of the school leavers' programme instead of an irrelevant extra. The National Curriculum means that schools have to be specific about what they want from a college link. SKILL have pointed out that the development of a successful partnership must involve agreement and co-operation to facilitate joint planning. Schools need to clarify their curricular objectives; colleges need to negotiate aims, teaching methods, contents and resourcing of courses prior to commencement of the course. Colleges need to offer a clear curriculum statement of the course framework, evaluation and review procedures, feedback and record keeping so that communication is enhanced, negotiation kept flexible and practices shared and modified (Corbett 1990). Adequate funding must be available to ensure transport to and from college and to facilitate access to a range of departmental resources. Use of regional consortia will facilitate bargaining on both parts and allow greater choice. Schools should provide adequate time and resources for the transition process, as should colleges of further education.

Courses need to be validated where possible and this process may be facilitated by the use of Records of Achievement which could be used to contribute to the National Curriculum documentation and also to provide evidence for the accreditation of prior learning (DES 1991; Corbett, 1990). In some areas modular units have been accredited by regional examination boards. Functional integration must be provided and above all students should have an entitlement to progression. What should not be forgotten is the end of the process, which is to equip the student for living in the community with confidence to interact with others, knowing how to access and participate in local social activities (McGinty and Fish 1992).

Some of the tasks that can be undertaken by schools have been summarised by John Fish:

> ...courses should be reviewed to take account of changing social patterns and employment prospects. This demands that teachers are well informed about prospects for further education, vocational and social training, employment and living conditions. They need to know the criteria used by other institutions and agencies for admission to courses and the range of services available to those who are handicapped after leaving school. It is necessary to see the final years of schooling as the beginning of the transition process and not as an end to education. (1985)

Other commentators have suggested that school preparation should begin at thirteen plus when choices have to be made. It is likely that the school pupils are in at this age is the one they will finish their education in. It is also the age at which TVEI begins and the statutory age when the 1981 Act requires attention to review and assessment for statements (McGinty and Fish 1992) .

McGinty and Fish have suggested that the process of school reasssesment at thirteen plus for a future programme should result in a comprehensive transition plan being drawn up. The transition plan should be forward looking, covering the whole of the transition and capable of review and modification. It should start with a resumé of an individual's educational, medical, social and work experience and set out a series of goals based on opportunities in the school and the neighbourhood. These goals should include the skills and knowledge to be acquired for further education and training, independent living, open or supported employment, recreation, leisure and social interaction with the community (McGinty and Fish 1992). For a young visually-impaired person this should also include familiarisation with the technology and systems that will facilitate effective communication in further education (Vincent 1989). The American Individual Transition plan might act as a useful basis for local initiatives in this area (Wehman et al, 1988 and Sailor et al, 1989). It would certainly provide a foundation for the vital practice of keeping and transferring records before, during and after transition.

Colleges also have a contribution to make which will in turn enable others to work effectively in transition. An entitlement curriculum which emphasises the study, communication and interpersonal skills that will be vital if a student is to be effective in further education should be considered for all colleges and should be further developed where it already exists. Guidance and counselling that is available when and where the individual needs it is important, and it should also inform the whole system of support for that student, whether it be a personal tutor system or a mentor system. Effective initial and ongoing assessment will help to provide programmes of study and support which will consequently allow the individual to fulfil their potential. Colleges should also be aware of the support that is available to them in meeting the needs of the students, whether this be in local schools, local and national voluntary agencies such as the RNIB student support services and SKILL, or Access and other specialist centres. McGinty (1992) has also suggested that colleges should undertake an audit of provision to see whether they are fully meeting the transitional needs of the visually-impaired customer (FEU 1989).

Further education and schools can greatly facilitate the transition process for young visually-impaired people – and there are many examples of good practice that have been developed throughout the country – but they cannot solely be responsible. Nor are schools and colleges obvious co-ordinating agencies. Co-operation with others is vital but difficult to establish in the absence of an established framework and lack of recognition by management of the importance of such a framework. As McGinty has observed 'each authority, each local area and each neighbourhood will have to consider transition and evolve a pattern of opportunities and choices from which to fashion individual transition plans' (1992). Until they do so the tremendous potential that young visually-impaired people have to contribute to and personally grow from opportunities in further education will be dissipated by the unsuccessful or partial transition which often means that only the fittest survive.

40

References

Adams, J.D., Hayes, J. and Hopson, B. (1976) *Transition: understanding and managing personal change* (London: Martin Robertson).

Corbett, J. (1990) *No longer enough: developing the curriculum in special school/college link courses* (SKILL: London).

DES (24/91/NS) (1991) *Transition from school to further education for students with learning difficulties* (DES: London).

FEU (1986) *Transition to Adulthood* (FEU: London).

FEU (1989) *Towards an Educational Audit* (FEU: London).

Fish, J. (1985) *Special Education: the way ahead* (OUP: Milton Keynes).

Hinds, D. (1991) *Report to research and development steering committee* (NAIMS/NATSPEC).

McGinty, J. and Fish, J. (1992) *Learning Support for Young People in Transition* (OUP: Buckingham).

Sailor, W., Anderson, D.L., Halvorsen, Ed.D., Doering, K., Filler and Goetz., L. (1989) *The Local Comprehensive School* (Baltimore: Paul H Brookes).

Vincent, A.T. (1989) *New Technology, Disability and Special Educational Needs* (Coventry: Empathy Ltd).

Wehman, P., Moon, M.S., Everson, J.M., Wood, W. and Barcus, J.M. (1988) *Transition from School to Work* (Baltimore: Paul H Brookes).

CHAPTER FOUR

Support Services in an Integrated Setting

Paul Lynch

The Tertiary Service for Students with a Visual Impairment (TSSVI) was formally established in September, 1988 within the framework of Sheffield's unified tertiary system. The Service, based at Loxley College (now the Loxley Centre of the Sheffield College), operates throughout all the city's post-sixteen centres, supporting students with a severe visual impairment on courses of their choice. In addition to the full range of mainstream courses available, students can opt for dedicated courses in braille or cookery. Before long the area of operation extended to Sheffield Polytechnic (now Sheffield Hallam University) and Sheffield University.

History

In 1981 Sheffield City Council began formally to review provision for post-primary education (but not including Sheffield City Polytechnic). The review, whose report was published in 1985, was prompted by a number of factors: mainly to 'manage and safeguard the quality of educational opportunity for those age groups affected by rapid demographic change' to 'provide and facilitate access to ... continuing education and training opportunities for young people and adults' and to consider the participation rate in post-compulsory education.

The review established six clear aims including the following

(iii) Integration of People with Special Needs.
To integrate, as far as is feasible, children, young people and adults with special educational needs within school, college and community-based provision.

After consultation and consideration of all the alternatives the

Authority decided in 1982 to reorganise all maintained post-sixteen education based on a unified system of tertiary colleges. It also opted to reorganise secondary schools so as to retain as local a base as possible with due regard to the range and quality of provision. Under the original plan the eight tertiary colleges would subsume the work of the existing colleges of further education, the adult education services and the sixth forms of secondary schools. The plan ultimately approved by the Secretary of State for Education permitted certain schools to retain their sixth forms and six new tertiary colleges were to be formed. (From September 1992, these amalgamated to form the Sheffield College.)

This was a huge undertaking as there were 35 county secondary schools, five colleges of further education and eleven adult education divisions. In order to implement the aims of the review, a working party was established to prepare the reorganisation plan. This was a large group with many representatives and it was ultimately agreed to form small task groups to concentrate on specific issues and for these to report back to the Working Party. One group was established to look at 'provision for pupils/students with special educational needs' and this group became known as the Special Needs Advisory Committee.

The Special Needs Advisory Committee (SNAC) had as its draft terms of reference to assist the Chief Education Officer through:

- the identification of needs and the monitoring of provision;
- advice on resources and access;
- the fostering of a multi-professional approach to provision;
- the identification of staff and curriculum development needs.

SNAC began with a wide representation of those concerned with special needs provision. It was agreed at the first meeting of the group that membership could be expanded to ensure that any interests not represented could be included. As it evolved the group had members representing:

- People with disabilities and/or their advocates
- Schools and colleges
- Family and Community Services (Social Services)
- Careers, Medical and Psychological Services
- Manpower Services Commission Training Division
- The Education Department.

The group anticipated meeting four times a year and duly made representations to the Chief Education Officer. When the proposals for reorganisation were published they contained the recommendation for 'the establishment of an integrated resource for post-sixteen visually handicapped students'. This new support service was to be based at a college in close proximity to the existing provision for pupils with a visual impairment in the Open Education Scheme operated via Tapton Mount School at Tapton Comprehensive. Consequently Loxley College became the base of the Tertiary Service for Students with a Visual Impairment.

Implementation of the recommendations

Although students were not due in the new colleges until September 1988, a considerable planning stage was well under way prior to that date. A report submitted to SNAC in 1987 regarding the needs of students with a visual impairment detailed the requirements of an adequately resourced service which was to operate across the city not only in the six main sites of the new colleges but in any of the many neighbourhood centres.

This report outlined the need for appropriate staff levels, specialist equipment and general accommodation requirements. The staff team was envisaged to consist of support/peripatetic lecturer(s), rehabilitation officer(s) and technician(s) and where possible those appointed should have relevant experience/qualifications in dealing with the needs of students with a visual impairment.

With its inception in September 1988, the Service began with one full-time support lecturer (qualified to teach those with a visual impairment), two part-time lecturers for the discrete classes and a resources budget.

In the academic year prior to the start date, the first expected intake of students numbered five (three full-time) studying across the city. In addition, the part-time braille and cookery classes were expecting ten and six students respectively. It was pointed out in the report to SNAC that the experience of services in other parts of the country was one of rapid growth in student numbers and this has proved to be the case. By the actual launch of the Service in September 1988, the numbers had already grown by a further two full-time and six part-time students. This was only to be expected in a city the size of Sheffield (population approximately 530,000) coupled with the fact that the new post-sixteen provision included the former Adult Education Divisions (the vast majority of people with a visual impairment being aged 40+).

In September 1992 the Service knew of 60+ students throughout the further and higher education system. The staff team expanded accordingly to total three full-time lecturers (all qualified to teach people with a visual impairment), four part-time lecturers, a qualified rehabilitation officer and a technician.

Mode of operation

The Service works on the basic premise of supporting students on courses of their choice. The range of subjects on offer throughout the further and higher education system is vast and different centres and sites do have particular specialisms (e.g. catering, engineering, journalism). So students are established in a large number of centres. Students exercise this fundamental right to choose largely on a basis of personal subject preference at an appropriate level and where possible at a convenient geographical location. Consequently the Service has to be a very mobile one when offering support.

For a student with a visual impairment to select, join and eventually complete a particular course, implies potential involvement of the Service well in advance of any course actually beginning. This in turn requires a means by which an individual knows of the Service and vice versa. There are a number of channels by which information is distributed or obtained regarding the Service or potential students. The means varies, and can depend on whether or not the individual is a school leaver, known to the Careers Service, known to Family and Community (Social) Services or possibly none of these.

The Service has strong links with the schools sector and as a visually-impaired pupil enters his/her final year, this information is passed on, usually by a member of the support team working in the secondary area. TSSV then becomes part of the planning process. Similar arrangements exist with the Careers Service and information and awareness raising sessions are organised for officers of that department. Meetings are held (usually on a monthly basis) with the rehabilitation team from Family and Community Services where the information flow is very much a two-way process.

Details of the existence of the Service are contained in general College literature, in a particular booklet describing the whole range of provision for students with any special educational need (SCOPE) and in a Service leaflet which is available in various formats. Local radio and 'Talking News' tape services can provide a ready-made link for those for whom the printed word is not readily accessible.

For potential students contacting any centre or site of the College directly, there are means of ensuring appropriate details are passed to the Service and vice versa. Each main centre of the College (six in all) has a special needs co-ordinator to whom reference is made by course or admissions teams should an individual declare a particular educational need. The co-ordinators then inform the Service of any students with a visual impairment. The role of special needs co-ordinator is a vital one as detailed knowledge of their particular centre (and neighbourhood sites) with respect to staff, courses, layout and general facilities helps to establish valuable links rapidly between the individual and the College. In addition there is then a permanent contact point at each main centre to whom needs can be addressed, should the Service not be in that particular centre when that need arises.

Assessing support

Once a potential student is known to the Service, a member of the team will usually arrange a personal visit to establish the individual's requirements with respect to:-

- preferred work medium/media (braille, print, tape etc)
- types of course details
- preferred college/locations
- mobility/travel
- equipment
- classroom/individual support from TSSV
- individual tutorial from subject specialist(s)

Course details are then provided in an appropriate format.

Moving on

Informal visit(s) are arranged to the relevant centre(s) should an individual so wish and the opportunity then arises to gather further details of a particular course from the teaching staff involved. At the same time the specific needs of that individual can then become known to the staff concerned. An unpressurised, casual visit can help elicit more valuable knowledge of a student's requirements than a more formal interview.

Implementing support

Should a person be offered and accept a place on a course then any further action by TSSV is governed by the wishes of that individual, the details of the needs previously assessed and any additional requirements expressed by course delivery staff. The range of support offered can cover a wide spectrum of involvement depending on the choice and nature of the course to be followed.

Classroom support

After due consultation with the student and class lecturer, the support lecturer works alongside the student to facilitate maximum participation in class activities. The areas in which support is given include not only the everyday class or lecture room but also more specialist areas such as science laboratories, information technology suites and home economics rooms. With a student on a horticulture course, the workplace was the glasshouse, the potting shed and the open fields.

Most students on full-time courses have the option of a leisure orientated programme. As a consequence the support team members have been found in a huge range of pursuits from archery and athletics to ski-ing, swimming and windsurfing.

Additional individual support

In this instance the support lecturer works on a one-to-one basis with the student. This may be with regard to coursework and it may include topics specific to the individual, possibly the development of communication skills (such as Braille or typing) or the use of specialised equipment and software.

Rehabilitation officer support

The range of study opportunities open to students with a visual impairment would be greatly curtailed (if not completely expunged) without the input of a qualified rehabilitation officer. The need for safe, independent travel to and from the place(s) of study as well as in and around campus is fundamental to a student's well-being. The greatest challenge to the student, on a daily basis, should be the subject matter, not the journey to college.

The rehabilitation officer will assess the student's mobility needs and skills (these can be enhanced where necessary). All relevant journeys will be planned and taught as appropriate. The relatively quiet time during college holidays is often made use of by way of introduction to particular routes. In addition the teaching of communication and life skills can give the student confidence and can alleviate difficulties that would inhibit taking up the further challenges inherent in studying.

Adaptation of materials

It has been asserted that eighty percent of learning is via the visual pathway. This puts a great emphasis on the appropriate adaptation of the vast amount of 'visual material' routinely used during lectures. Depending on the preferences of an individual student, information may be required in braille, Moon, print (of a suitable size and clarity), audio format, tactile diagrams, maps and models or any combination of these. The amount of such material from city-wide sources requires the services of a skilful and resourceful technician.

The production of this adapted material involves the use of a range of low to high technology equipment. Hand frames, mechanical braillers and a vacuum-forming machine are used side by side with a scanner, computers and a braille embosser. The output of adapted text, either into braille or suitable print, is greatly speeded up if the original material is obtainable in electronic file format. With so many publishers and individual lecturers making use of word-processing techniques, together with the development of the 'electronic' book, newspaper and the compact disk, the volume of accessible up-to-date material for students with a visual impairment has increased enormously.

In-service training/awareness raising

With visual impairment being statistically much less frequent than other causes giving rise to special educational needs, it is likely that most college staff will be unfamiliar with many aspects of the condition. Fundamental then, to successful integration is the guidance offered to staff and fellow students by the Service.

A dilemma arises in the fact that some of the most vital people to contact, namely the subject specialists, are often the most difficult to muster in one spot – largely because of teaching commitments and the problems associated with cover arrangements. Consequently, although the in-service program has set sessions the college staff can attend, it is very productive for TSSVI members to attend course delivery or team meetings where the relevant staff would normally be gathered.

A typical in-service session would include:

- explanation of the phrase 'visual impairment' and dealing with the popular concept of 'blindness';
- details of different eye conditions and, in particular, their impact on the accessibility (or otherwise) of printed text;
- discussion of the educational implications of a severe visual impairment;
- strategies for minimising the potential handicapping effect of a particular eye condition. For instance, ensuring that wherever possible, as course materials are distributed to the class, the same materials are available at the same time and in a suitable format for the student with sight difficulties;
- instructions on how to guide a blind person (sighted guide technique).

A simplified version of the above can be used to raise the awareness of fellow members of the class. These sessions are arranged with the collaboration and co-operation of the student concerned. Indeed some individuals have actively participated in them and have found it useful to relay information, at one stroke, to all that need to know of their situation and specific needs.

Technical tutorial

A valuable contribution to the satisfactory progress of some students with a visual impairment has been the willingness of course delivery teams to arrange a technical tutorial (usually on a weekly basis). Here the student receives an individual tutorial from a course lecturer in his/her specialist subject. It is a very useful opportunity for the student to pick up on any information or details that have not been fully absorbed during the usual class period – often because of the pace of delivery coupled with the volume of material. The time-tabling and financial implications of such tutorials are significant; however, equally important is the benefit they can bring.

Loan of equipment

The Service has a wide range of 'low-tech' to 'high-tech' equipment for students to borrow for the duration of their course. The range includes braille rulers, graph boards and lamps, tape recorders, electric typewriters and talking calculators; voice synthesisers, closed-circuit televisions and stand alone electronic braille-input devices.

Use of the equipment obtained by the Service has a number of facets. Primarily this has been to enable the student to partake as fully as possible within a given lesson by overcoming some of the constraints of the visual problem. For example, by using text enhancing software in a word processing course, a partially-sighted student can have immediate access to the same commercial computer packages as the rest of the class.

Appropriate equipment, confidently used, can also make the student independent of continuous classroom support from the Service, thereby enabling support to be offered to a growing number of people. A device and printer attached to a brailler gives a translated version of any brailled work. In an English class, for instance, the student would have their tactile notes whilst the device would output, via the printer, a version that can be marked and assessed by the mainstream class teacher.

The very specific nature of some of the equipment in use by the students means that it can be very expensive. For most students this cost may prevent them undertaking some courses. If the Service has the equipment, there is no such bar to the student. Those people who might, in the long term wish to own such items have the opportunity to test the equipment's suitability over a long period, without a large outlay of funds at the outset. Making use of Service equipment can help an informed judgement to be made.

Much consideration needs to be given regarding the provision of necessary, but non-portable, equipment. It can transpire that some students require the use of such apparatus in a number of locations: home (or hall of residence), classroom(s) in various buildings and libraries. Obtaining multiples of these units may be necessary – all strategically placed.

For some pieces of equipment, time and training needs to be available for students to establish competent and confident use. These items require much sophistication in their use and appropriate coaching is vital if they are not to become a source of frustration. Indeed, the skills needed in the application of such items can be as intricate as those to be acquired by their use in the first place. The Service has an important role to play in this area.

It may well transpire that at some time during a course a student makes use of the previous support structure, to a greater or lesser degree. Consequently the Service sees as important its role in the planning process and in liaising with students, parents where necessary, college staff, medical and careers personnel. Early notification of an application by a student with a visual impairment means that the optimum structure of support can be ascertained and made available.

Case studies

The huge range of courses at the disposal of the students are usually taught by mainstream lecturers with the backing of administrative teams, ancillary staff, librarians and technicians. All play a key role in the delivery of courses. The combination of their expertise with the specialist knowledge of TSSVI members provides a sound basis on which successful integration and effective learning can be established.

Case A

Among the first intake of students supported by the Service, was a school leaver intending to follow a BTEC National course. In the autumn term prior to leaving school, plans were laid for the transition to further education. Staff development was arranged for the course team. The reading list for the course was analysed in conjunction with the subject specialists and the most vital books not already available in braille or on tape were transcribed by the Wakefield Prison Braille Unit. Course notes were brailled by the support lecturer and other local experienced braillists. Mobility was arranged with a qualified mobility teacher via the service at Tapton Mount. A number of Perkins braillers were placed in the various centres to be used; adapted weighing scales and braille recipes were available in the domestic science department; a voice synthesiser and screen reading software was installed in the computer room. Intensive classroom support was arranged during the mathematics, domestic science and word processing options and continued throughout the course. The planning process was repeated to take account of a work experience placement. The course was successfully completed.

Case B

A would-be student contacted the Service having heard of its existence by word of mouth. During a home visit, the myriad of opportunities, and the support available was outlined. The individual concerned then made all the necessary contacts with the college and went on to successfully complete a number of courses. After the initial contact, involvement of the Service was minimal save for being available in an advisory capacity and providing and maintaining equipment.

Case C

Given due notice, the Service has an established method of planning and development. However, not all applicants for courses apply well in advance. Such was the case here with the individual appearing mid-term at the college reception desk wanting to follow a course – any course! During a home visit, it was established that the purpose of studying was to lead to employment. Although a slight knowledge of braille was alluded to, the individual had no means of written communication. Consequently, individual typing lessons were arranged, enrolment in the braille class followed, and the individual also joined a pottery group (by request).

It soon became evident to the braille and typing teachers that the individual needed literacy tuition of a most basic nature. Consequently the skills of the adult education team in the college were much utilised in constructing an individual programme of learning taking cognisance of the person's lack of reading and braille competence. The joint approach of the Service and adult education specialists (together with the library team who have helped to establish a tape service) has meant very significant, albeit, gradual progress. This has culminated in the award of an accredited English certificate. The person continues with the individual programme, which now incorporates numeracy, with much one-to-one support, jointly provided.

External Agencies

As well as being in touch with all the local sources of help and information, the Service has regular contact with the RNIB Student Service and, with a view to progression, the RNIB Employment Network. Other agencies include The Partially Sighted Society, SKILL (National Bureau for Handicapped Students) and the FE Curriculum Group of the Association for the Education and Welfare of the Visually Handicapped/RNIB.

Further and Higher Education Act 1992

The passing of the above Act introduced a number of important reforms in the funding and organisation of further education and saw the establishment of the Further Education Funding Council (FEFC).

FEFC will "fund learning" and will allocate resources provided by the Secretary of State for courses falling within the remit of Schedule 2 of the Act. FEFC is required under section 4 of the Act to have regard to the requirements of students with 'learning difficulties and disabilities' and is committed to maintaining continuity of provision for such students. As a consequence, under the funding methodology (FEFC Circular 93/32), five bands of additional units/resources are available to meet the assessed needs of particular individuals.

September 1993 saw the start of work of the Learning Difficulties Committee, chaired by Professor J Tomlinson. The committee, set up by FEFC, has a three-year life and is to review the range and type of further education available (in England) to people with learning difficulties and disabilities, and to make recommendations to the Council. Amongst the committee's considerations will be:

- definition and assessment of students with learning difficulties
- the role of the special colleges
- funding, organisation and delivery of support services
- quality of provision

Conclusion

The role of supporting students in an integrated setting brings challenges that are varied and far-reaching. The wide variety of subject matter, the range of abilities, ages and experience of the students all combine to stretch and motivate TSSV staff to new and ever more diverse limits.

The Sheffield College offers in the first criteria of its mission statement: 'a comprehensive, consistent and high quality education and training service to customers of all ages, all interests and all abilities'. The opportunity for people to 'take responsibility for their own individual development' (Mission Statement), has much to do with that individual having the freedom to choose what, where and when to study. TSSV helps to ensure that opportunity is there for the students it supports in Sheffield.

References

Sheffield City Council (1985) *New Schools and Colleges: Proposals for the Reorganisation of Post-Primary Education.*
DFE (1992) *The Further and Higher Education Act* (HMSO)

CHAPTER FIVE

PICKUP Provision for the Visually-Impaired Client

Mary Bennett

PICKUP (Professional, Industrial and Commercial Updating Services) have steadily increased in mainstream further education colleges since 1982. PICKUP is aimed at offering adults in employment continuing vocational education in a wide range of skills and knowledge and can be delivered in a variety of ways.

It often takes the form of short courses, backed by training needs analysis and other consultancy services and increasingly has been related to national vocational qualifications. PICKUP services are usually priced at full cost and are paid for by the employer or the individual employee.

The Department of Education and Science (now the Department For Education) has encouraged the development of PICKUP with the longer-term aim of its recognition as an integral part of a college's range of activities. It is suggested that PICKUP should account for around 10% of a college's workload by 1992. Within mainstream further education the clients PICKUP have aimed to attract came mainly from local businesses and services. PICKUP provision is often tailor-made to the specific needs of a local company's workforce. Colleges have developed this provision along extensively commercial lines and PICKUP services are often referred to as Enterprise or Commercial Units, their business largely one of income generation for the college.

PICKUP services for the visually impaired, provided within a specialist further education college, are able to develop in a similar manner to only a limited extent. This is due in part to the numbers and geographical spread of the client group. In practical terms, the estimated numbers of employed adults with a visual impairment in Britain is around 22,000. This is probably less than the adult employed group of a large town in this country, and the spread is nationwide. The result of this is a very specialist service provision and one which has to take into account the many factors relating to the employment of visually-impaired people.

PICKUP provision for the visually impaired is available from a range of providers. This training has tended to concentrate on clients who have a long-standing sight loss and require an updating of their skills within existing commercial employment. This is a limited definition of visually-impaired people within employment and relies upon the individual being identified and registered as either blind or partially sighted.

The Office of Population and Census Services Disability Survey of 1989 identified that 31% of all disabled people under pensionable age were in paid employment. The RNIB's survey of 1991 found that amongst visually-impaired people the overall figure of those within employable age limits, in work was 25%. That figure represented 17% of registered blind and 31% of registered partially sighted people.

Indeed, the RNIB survey showed that not being in paid employment is normal for visually-impaired people, with approximately one in four visually-impaired people in work. The national figure of 22,000 adults is increased to 30,000 since a further 8,000 visually impaired people are still in work after normal retirement ages. These appear to be mainly female and part-time workers, who for reasons relating to pensions and so forth continue beyond the age of retirement.

Again, these figures relate to registered figures and can make no reference to individuals whose sight deteriorates within employment and who continue to work with or without assistance from their employers. Understandably in a recession an employee finding difficulty in working due to failing eyesight, may be reluctant to bring this to the attention of their employers.

The RNIB survey concludes that there is a link between the onset of visual impairment and the employee ceasing work. This is more apparent if this occurs within the first two years of employment and may relate to the parameters of employment legislation and unfair dismissal claims. However, it is fair to say that there is generally lower job mobility amongst visually-impaired employed people; once the employer/employee partnership is established over a longer period, the chances of long-term employment after onset of visual impairment can be good.

The survey also points out that employers are unaware of the rehabilitation and retraining services (for which they have to pay) and the Special Aids to Employment Scheme (for which they do not pay). It concludes that statutory and voluntary agencies should undertake much more significant public education campaigns aimed at employers, trade unions and employees to rectify this.

In the 1980s the Royal National College for the Blind (RNCB) at Hereford contracted with the Residential Training College Unit to provide Employment Training places for unemployed visually-impaired adults. This brought about a change in the age structure of the College from a predominantly 16–25 years range to one of 16–50 years, which has remained until the present.

The College is the largest vocational further education college for the visually impaired in the United Kingdom and is committed to supporting its students into employment or higher education. It offers National Vocational Qualifications in a wide range of subject areas and has developed an extensive work experience programme for its students in their own home areas.

As the College diversified its activities it became apparent that one client group not accessing training opportunities sufficiently were those visually-impaired adults in employment. The College Governors supported an application to the Further Education Unit (FEU) of the Department of Education and Science for a grant to pilot a PICKUP project in the West Midlands area. The FEU supported this application, a grant was made available, and in March 1990 a Project Officer was appointed.

The project aimed to investigate the training needs of visually-impaired clients who were unable to meet effectively new and/or existing demands upon them in employment, due to an existing or deteriorating level of sight. It was suggested in the project's abstract that the PICKUP needs of these clients were not being fully met at that time, but that through the development of both local and national provision this could be attained. This would be of mutual benefit for both employer and employee.

The project took eighteen months to complete and sought applicants to participate from the West Midlands area. Some 41 visually-impaired adults in employment expressed interest in PICKUP as a result of an awareness raising campaign and eight of these were selected for inclusion in the project.

The criteria for selection were: assessment of need, viability of programme, existing commercial employment, employer support and siting within the West Midlands region.

The model for training provision was based on the following:

- a multi-disciplinary assessment of the client;
- equipment and training needs analysis;
- client-centred training based upon a functional analysis of present employment and projected future work demands;
- monitoring of the project was provided by the Project Steering Committee and evaluation was both formative (through regular contact with the clients) and summative (through use of evaluation sheets).

Throughout the process, regular discussions with both the employer and employee were maintained. Training was delivered at the Royal National College for the Blind, or took the form of supported integrated training at a suitable college of further education or on site at the client's place of work.

The client group could be divided into two quite distinct categories. The first group were clients who had a long-standing but stable sight loss. PICKUP provision for this group enabled them to respond to new demands at work and helped towards career development and progression. The second group were those who had experienced a deterioration of sight whilst in employment. In this case issues raised often concerned the fear of loss of employment or of a lower grade alternative. This different perspective on PICKUP training still exists and in the light of the current recession is likely to remain an issue for a long time. The factors which affect an individual in employment are multidimensional and the level of sight an individual possesses is only one aspect. The working environ- ment, employers' and colleagues' attitudes, job specifications, training facilities, equipment available and its appropriate funding are all relevant in the provision of PICKUP services for the visually- impaired client.

The report concluded that irrespective of the nature, content and location of a client's training programme, the demand for support is constant and incorporates four distinct areas.

1. Needs analysis

This requires to be multi-disciplinary and on-going, and where appropriate could include an independent assessment of vision.

2. Co-ordination of advice and information

To include information on providers, funding, equipment and training. PICKUP training is often a multi-agency concern and needs a central point or person to draw it altogether.

3. Multi-disciplinary assessment

This needs to be properly co-ordinated, as must the work of the range of professionals who are involved with a client and their training programme. The technical aspect of the training programme requires the greatest amount of specialist knowledge.

4. Expertise in the field of commercially based technology

Knowledge of adaptations available for the visually impaired and the range of special equipment available are all required.

The report makes a number of recommendations based on the success of the project. Several of these relate to practical issues of how a nationwide PICKUP service could operate and these have been addressed by the College. The others are recommendations based on the general principles of whether a PICKUP service is a requirement for visually-impaired people in employment.

The report unequivocally recommends that a quality PICKUP training provision should be available to visually-impaired commercial employees in this country. Employers should be consulted at each stage and their needs as well as the clients' needs taken into account. A flexible training response should be available which will provide the employer and the client with a variety of options for training, to suit individual need. The report also indicates a significant demand for updating and retraining visually-impaired employees and concludes that at the time of publication there was little provision available to respond to these needs.

The research project focuses on those within employment currently experiencing deterioration of sight, but it also reveals a need to offer PICKUP services to those in work with an already established sight loss. Clearly, the needs of this category of person are linked, although not identical, with those studied in the research project.

The project ended in the summer of 1991 and the College, which is committed to expand and diversify its activities, decided to appoint a full-time PICKUP Development Officer to extend current college PICKUP services to a nationwide provision. The author was appointed and the initiative launched in January 1992.

In 1992 the Disablement Advisory Service was replaced by the new Placement, Assessment and Counselling Teams. Concurrently the Employment Rehabilitation Services (ERS)and Centres were replaced by nine Ability Development Centres throughout the country. This is in line with Government policy announced in April 1991 that over the next five years employment rehabilitation and assessment will progressively be taken out of the hands of the ERS and contracted out to external agents, including voluntary sector organisations. Changes in role and personnel have occurred in all regions at different rates, as Disability Employment Advisors (DEAs) have adjusted to their new responsibilities.

The DEAs are crucial in their role of assisting and supporting people into employment. The categories of disability are wide ranging and individual DEA's experience and knowledge of specific conditions is inevitably very variable. A specialist college has an important role in increasing awareness and knowledge of visual impairment with appropriate Employment Service staff and the RNCB enjoys a good working relationship with PAC Teams throughout the country.

The Employment Service, through its Placement, Assessment and Counselling Teams (PACTs) operates the Special Aids to Employment Scheme. This enables an employee to be assessed for and supplied with specialist equipment and facilities on free and permanent loan basis.

At the discretion of the PACT member, generally two or three days funded training can be made available to the employee in the use of the equipment. This is often insufficient and the project cited cases where expensive equipment was allocated to individuals, but no funding was made available to assist the employee to use it. Suppliers may offer training as part of the package when buying equipment but this is usually only a day in length and includes commissioning time. Employers are sometimes reluctant to purchase additional training for their staff member due to costs and in part due to a lack of specialist knowledge of the needs of their visually impaired employees.

In order to access help from the SAE Scheme an individual has to contact the PAC Team via the DEA at their local Job Centre. A client must apply for Registration under the 1944 Disabled Persons

(Employment) Act to access the facilities of the SAE Scheme. A special aid is defined as an 'item of equipment needed by a client with a disability which would not be needed by a non-disabled person'. Individuals may not always follow this pathway as registration is voluntary, and they may choose to fund their own specialist equipment or their employer may be prepared to fund this directly. Additionally there may be time delays in obtaining equipment from the PAC Team, or insufficient funding to provide all the equipment an individual wishes to use.

The new Access to Work Regulations will come into effect on April 1st, 1994. Their exact form is not yet clear, but indications are that employers will increasingly be required to contribute to the purchase and supply of specialist equipment and training for people with disabilities who are in employment.

PICKUP services involve a collaborative approach between client, employer and DEA. The SAE scheme should not be used by an employer as the sole staff development facility for a visually-impaired employee. Rather, it should be seen as the necessary support to employees to allow effective performance of work roles.

The design of PICKUP services is modelled on the traditional training cycle which involves four interlinked phases of activity (see figure 5.1). As with all cycles there is no defined beginning or end, it is a continuous process.

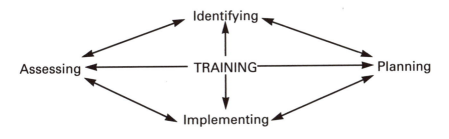

Figure 5.1

However, in practice training cannot operate in isolation and there needs to be a clear link to other activities within the organisation. Visually impaired employees should, can and do participate in any appropriate staff development activities within the organisation in the same way as their sighted colleagues. PICKUP services aim to offer a specialist training function when and where required to support the employer and employee and enable them to achieve organisational and individual goals.

Within the scope of the model outlined, the College has developed PICKUP services in three main areas.

1. Individual, tailor-made programmes designed to offer clients the facility to update their skills and knowledge in specific areas.
2. Technical updating, training and awareness raising on a wide range of equipment for both blind and partially-sighted people.
3. A short course programme available for visually-impaired people, carers, employers and professionals in the field of visually impairment.

The advances made in technology over recent years have certainly created many new opportunities for visually-impaired people. Updating skills can offer an employee more scope for personal and career development and increased job satisfaction. The employer benefits from a greater efficiency of work effort and development of an individual's potential.

However, it would be wrong to limit PICKUP services to the use of technology within the office environment. Visually-impaired people enjoy a wide range of occupations, as information produced by the RNIB's Small Business Unit and the Blind Business Association shows. The range of trade and service businesses run by visually-impaired people includes activities in all fields, and incorporates a large element of self-employment for visually-impaired people.

For those in employment PICKUP training may be funded either by the Employment Services, via the PAC Teams, or by the employer. The self-employed are in a different funding category to some extent and have the options of self-financing their training, gaining funding from their DEA or via their local Training and Enterprise Council (TEC). TECs around the country vary considerably in their approach to the funding of initiatives like PICKUP and to the level of support for disability employment matters in general. The College has experienced some success in gaining funding from local TECs and this is an area that will be developed further.

Many self-employed visually-impaired businessmen and women use technology to their advantage in areas such as their accountancy systems, business correspondence and client databases. The College has for some years run a Small Business course for its students who leave to become self-employed in areas such as piano tuning and remedial therapy. PICKUP is now drawing on this expertise to develop programmes to assist self-employed clients who are already established in business.

Through individual programmes and short courses PICKUP has developed on a College wide basis. Inevitably information technology and allied subjects form a major part of PICKUP work but the College aims to support visually-impaired employees in a wide variety of work areas and professions.

PICKUP clients are from a variety of occupational areas and are referred to PICKUP services in many different ways. To date around half of the current clients have been referred by their DEAs for assistance under the SAE scheme. The remainder are referred from other sources and a good proportion are self-referrals who require very specific help, support and advice.

Each PICKUP client is unique. Although they may present as requiring training with a word processing package or new piece of technology, their needs and the needs of their employment circumstances are highly individual and need to be addressed with this in mind.

PICKUP training at RNCB is primarily client-centred and delivered in a flexible way which suits the clients and their employers. The venue for delivery may be at the College in Hereford or on site at the client's workplace. Technical backup as well as tutorial support are essential and the College aims to provide both. The result is a high quality specialist provision, but, it must be said, this has financial implications and organisational consequences for the client and the College.

The development of a PICKUP service alongside the main business of the College, which is the provision of specialist further education to visually-impaired people, is not without its administrative difficulties.

Inevitably the needs of PICKUP to be responsive and flexible to client requirements can result in time-tabling difficulties and conflicting demands on the time of tutoring and technical staff. PICKUP services are available throughout the year and this has required the staff involved to work through College holiday periods. Staff commitment and enthusiasm for this service is very positive and the development of PICKUP Services has continued apace.

There is also an important element of staff development as a result of PICKUP Services. Word processing and integrated packages are constantly coming onto the commercial market and the College staff need to be familiar with the market leaders at any time and aware of their compatibility with speech and character enhancement facilities. Indeed there is a demand for many variations on a theme with this particular aspect and so tutorial and technical staff need to be able to offer a variety of training packages to respond to client requests. The same is true of developments in technology and equipment generally. On site training and workplace based assessments have meant more contact with the 'world of employment' for staff and the benefits of this are passed onto the College's full-time students.

PICKUP complements the College's existing work experience placements and as a recent College seminar named 'Into Employment and Beyond' reflected, provides a natural continuation for students into employment and support for future career development in the years ahead. PICKUP has thus become a natural progression of existing College facilities.

The PICKUP report defined its two main groups of clients: first, those with a long-standing but stable sight loss; second, those who had experienced a deterioration of sight whilst in employment. It is fair to say at this time that the majority of PICKUP clients so far have come from the first group. There have been notable exceptions; clients who have been part of the second group and whose employers have asked for help and advice at an early stage, recognising their employee was or would soon be experiencing difficulties due to visual impairment.

This is a complex but important area to deal with. The reality is that one in four registered blind or partially sighted people is in employment. The recession has hit all areas of commerce and industry and job mobility is low. However, the costs (both in financial and social terms) incurred in supporting a disabled person and perhaps their family within the state benefit system are well documented. This perhaps gives further support to the suggestion of a wider use by employers of disability leave for those members of staff who require it.

Disability leave can be defined as a period of time off work for a newly-disabled person, or a disabled person whose condition has deteriorated, during which their job is protected. In essence it is similar to maternity leave, except that provision is enshrined in employment legislation. The RNIB has produced a Guide to Employers on the subject of disability leave and is advocating a job protection scheme for people who become disabled whilst in employment and need time and support to make a proper assessment for their future.

Since the College launched its PICKUP initiative in 1992, there has been a steadily increasing rate of clients requiring tailor-made updating and technical training. This has indeed proved the conclusions of the project report that there is a need for a quality, national PICKUP service. The College aims to continue to develop this service.

PICKUP services require the College to be responsive, flexible and accessible to its clients. Implementation also requires close collaboration between employers, tutors and technical staff.

As a specialist further education college, the Royal National College for the Blind has an important role in increasing awareness among employers of the needs of visually-impaired people in employment. Building upon networks already formed will allow easier identification of clients whose sight is deteriorating whilst they are in employment. This will access PICKUP services to the client group who are currently under-represented in its take up.

The SAE scheme exists to support disabled people into employment, but the training requirements of a company's personnel are the responsibility of that company. This is no less true for disabled employees and employers need to be encouraged to increase their understanding and knowledge of the needs of the members of their workforce who are visually impaired or who may become so during their period of employment.

Accessing PICKUP services is an important aspect of creating equal opportunities for visually-impaired people within employment and will provide a challenging and worthwhile future development for the College.

References

Allen, D. and Etheridge, D.T (1991) *Commercial updating and training of employees experiencing a handicapping loss of sight whilst in commercial employment* (unpublished) Available from the FEU.

Bruce, I., Kennell, A. and Walker, E. (1991) *Blind and Partially Sighted Adults in Britain: The RNIB Survey* (HMSO).

Finn, D. (1992) *Disability or Health Problems, A Guide to Employment Services and Schemes* (YOUTHAID).

Martin, J., White, A. and Meltzer, H. (1989) *Disabled Adults:*

Services, Transport and Employment. O.P.C.S. Survey of Disability in Great Britain. Report 4 (HMSO).

Thomas, D. (1990) *Implementing PICKUP in LEA Colleges under the Education Reform Act 1988* (Further Education Unit)

Acknowledgements

The author wishes to thank the staff of the Further Education Unit for co-operation in reproduction of parts of FEU/PICKUP Project 597 in this chapter.

CHAPTER SIX

Competence: Myth or Reality?

Pauline Jeffrey

Competence – the word of the '90s. It has appeared once more as we are in the grips of recession and our unemployment levels are at a peak. We seem to feel the need today, as we have done in the past, to use competence whenever we need to demonstrate the ability of the British workforce to be the best and the most able to succeed. Therefore let us define 'competence'. The *Modern University Dictionary* states that the word 'competence' refers to the state of being fit or capable – properly qualified – legitimate. The National Council for Vocational Qualifications states that 'competence' is 'the ability to perform in a realistic working environment'. This is a wide concept which embodies skill transfer and a broad enough knowledge base to deal with new situations within an occupational area. It must incorporate the ability to plan, organise and deal with unpredictable occurrences. It must also demonstrate the ability to work within the culture of an organisation and with one's colleagues, supervisors, managers and customers.

The National Council for Vocational Qualifications was set up by the government following the White Paper 'Working Together: Education and Training' of July, 1986. It was set nine specific tasks:

I. Secure standards of occupational competence and ensure that vocational qualifications are based on them.
2. Design and implement a new national framework for vocational qualifications.
3. Approve bodies making accrediting awards.
4. Obtain comprehensive coverage of all occupational sectors.
5. Secure arrangements for quality assurance.
6. Set up effective liaison with bodies awarding vocational qualifications.
7. Establish a national database for vocational qualifications.
8. Undertake, or arrange to be undertaken, research and development to discharge these functions.

9. Promote vocational education, training and qualifications.

(NCVQ – the purpose and aims. NCVQ 1987)

A major part of these nine tasks was to secure standards of occupational competence. In order to do this the Industry Lead Bodies issued a code of practice for standards development. The key features of this standards development work are:

- Competence should enable the assessment of performance and should define achievement in terms of output.
- Each element of competence requires clearly defined performance criteria which define the performance.
- Elements of competence should be grouped into units of competence for certification purposes.
- The units should be packages which make sense and are valued in the context of employment.
- Suitable processes of assessment and verification will need to be established to ensure the credibility of vocational qualifications.
- Where feasible, performance in the workplace should be the basis of that assessment.

(TAG guidance note 1: a code of practice and a development model.
MSC, May 1988)

If we take into consideration these features with respect to a visually-impaired student we must understand their implications and the requirements in order to design a programme of training and assessment that will facilitate competence.

How do we achieve competence?

In the simplest of terms and using National Vocational Qualifications as a method of achieving this, we must begin our research in specialist colleges for the visually-impaired student. The first area for concern is to develop the understanding of the staff within these colleges in terms of today's definition of competence and how as teachers they must now change the emphasis to workbased learning and assessment. It has become a requirement of the National Council for Vocational Qualifications that students must not only understand the theory and be able to gain a qualification through examination, but also be able to demonstrate their ability to apply the knowledge and understanding in the workplace (the ability to perform). Because of these changes many colleges of further education, both mainstream and specialist, are having to embark upon the process of planned and accountable staff development. This will enable the staff to examine the process of work-based training and assessment and also become skilled in its application.

How do we assess – and to what standard?

We now have standards laid down by industry for industry. These were decided upon by Industry Lead Bodies as mentioned in the code of practice. These bodies include organisations such as the Engineering Industry Training Board, Construction Industry Training Board, Administrative, Business and Commercial Training Group, and the Training Development Lead Body who are now responsible for the national standards for all staff delivering training and assessment in the workplace. Similar Lead Bodies are currently establishing standards throughout vocational education and training both for the students and the teaching staff. A functional analysis of each sector was carried out across the country to establish these standards and they became what are known to us now as performance criteria.

These standards/performance criteria are a new concept to many colleges of further education and therefore a programme of training must be embarked upon to enable staff to carry out training and assessment to standards. What methods of assessment are to be applied in order to justify competence? There are three basic methods: observation of an activity, guided discussion and production of product evidence. Any assessment strategy must include these three methods. Why? Because if it can be demonstrated through a mixture of these methods that a student has the underpinning knowledge, the skill and the ability to apply these in a working environment, s/he is also demonstrating effectiveness within the workforce.

This process may be breaking down barriers for visually-impaired students. Had they been able to follow this process of assessment in the past, they would have been able to recognise their own achievements and the ability to transfer those achievements into a valuable contribution to the skill area they had chosen. In order for this assessment process to work, the delivery of the knowledge and understanding becomes paramount, along with the resources needed to facilitate it. So how do we establish a provision of aid and equipment to enable equal opportunity of access within a highly competitive marketplace? A massive cost implication appears at this stage to be an almost insurmountable barrier to colleges who have visually-impaired students. However, the mountainous cost of adaptation, once seemingly impossible, having been analysed against equal opportunity of access, may diminish to a molehill with the help of fund raising, making prospective employers more aware, and a little help from the government.

We appear to be on our way – or are we? A further area for concern at this point is time scale. How long does it take to achieve these qualifications in order to begin to plan? Because they are student-centred and focus on the needs of the individual there are no hard and fast rules on the length of time of study. This poses planning problems for colleges as we now know them. It means that no longer are they able to offer the same course structures and resources as before. They have now to focus far more on the individual learning plan, which allows the students to achieve at their own pace and in their own learning style. Additionally, and perhaps more importantly, funding will determine the length and level of the course undertaken by each student thereby restricting freedom of choice and equal access. Insistence on one-year funding by TECs has made access to higher level BTEC and other longer courses difficult.

Does the system work ?

The system *does* work but there is still a need to educate employers. They need to be made aware that when a student has achieved competence s/he has demonstrated this in a real working environment and has been able to deal with all that environment demands. The certificate does not imply competence but justifies it. A student may have the need for adapted equipment, but as the National Council for Vocational Qualifications stated 'Equal opportunities of access should form part of any system of qualifications'. The adaptation of equipment meets this requirement and becomes a tool of the trade and not an aid to competence. Many people in the past have feared that because a person has a visual impairment, uses adapted equipment and has gained a qualification through examination, s/he would not necessarily be as effective within the workforce. With the introduction of competence-based training and its assessment methods, we can at last demonstrate without reservation to employers that the qualification not only implies but also demonstrates and confirms competence in the workplace within a specific vocational area. Because students have been afforded equal status by being assessed at the same level, using the same assessment methods as others, they can demonstrate that they can be equally effective within the workplace. Many of these skills are core, common to many occupational areas and are therefore transferable throughout a variety of occupational areas.

At first glance and without having an in-depth understanding of competence-based training and assessment it may seem impossible for a visually-impaired student to achieve these standards. Therefore I embarked on the process of asking 'Is it possible?' The reactions were at first concern about the issues raised here such as timescale; funding adaptation of equipment; qualified training and assessment staffing; and a need for a higher level of understanding by employers. There was also a feeling that there is still a general misconception that a person with an impairment cannot be as competent as someone without a disability. However, after embarking on the process itself and being afforded equal opportunity of access, equal status within assessment and the availability of demonstrating competence in real working situations, a feeling of personal achievement was the result. Having broken down the barriers of traditional vocational qualifications, methods of teaching and assessment and prospective employer awareness, the ability to achieve became realistic.

What do these competencies look like?

Two units of competence may serve to demonstrate the nature and format of the competencies and their related performance criteria. This section also identifies how these units are achievable by a student with a visual impairment.

The following examples are taken from the national standards within the Administrative, Business and Commercial Training Group which were put forward for approval at levels one, two and three within the framework for National Vocational Qualifications.

UNIT TITLE: Telecommunications
ELEMENT: Operate a multiline/switchboard telephone system
PERFORMANCE CRITERIA:

- Calls are answered promptly and clearly using approved organisational manner.
- Callers identified and requirements established.

- Incoming calls always transferred appropriately or message passed on as appropriate.
- Correct external telephone calls always obtained and contact established or appropriate action taken.
- Courteous and helpful manner used at all times.
- Faults reported promptly.
- Operating and safety procedures are followed at all times.

If we carry out an analysis of the underpinning skills and knowledge required by the student to be able to demonstrate competence in the unit and the equipment needed to facilitate this it would be as follows

SKILLS

- Use directories (scanning devices; transcription into braille and large print; using 192 directory enquiries; magnification, devices, etc.).
- Operate switchboard (equipment adaptations can be provided by PACTs and modifications such as tactile representation and cueing devices).
- Listen to and interpret information.
- Speak clearly.
- React appropriately to requests and complaints.
- Liaise with colleagues and clients.
- Offer assistance to colleagues and clients.
- Write legible, logical messages (using typescript; word-processing software such as soft window enlargement of screen; audio representation of screen information, braille word-processing producing a print copy; and if all else fails either braille or handwritten shorthand for later transcription).
- Communicate effectively.

KNOWLEDGE

- Structure, location and responsibilities of people in organisation.
- Operation and facilities of system.
- British Telecom directories, codes, internal directories.
- Messaging forms.
- Range of British Telecom services and appreciation of costs.

- Common faults and their symptoms/routine cleaning and hygiene.
- Organisation's policy on telephone calls.
- Policy and procedures on security; safety and emergencies (e.g. bomb threats).

UNIT TITLE: Administrative support
ELEMENT: Carry out planning and booking procedures
PERFORMANCE CRITERIA:

- Plans/arrangements accurately reflect requirements and are consistent with organisational policy.
- Arrangements (travel, hotels etc.) are always confirmed in writing.
- Details of arrangements plus necessary documents presented in good time.

SKILLS
- Collect information from a variety of sources (scanning devices; access to disc using appropriate software and/or voice synthesis; transcription into appropriate form; use of readers; use of audio data).
- Extract and interpret relevant information from a variety of sources (see above).
- Plan collation and presentation of information and documents.
- Approximate/estimate from given data.
- Use a calculator (calculators with either enlarging screen or voice synthesis).
- Calculate British and foreign currency.
- Compose letters of confirmation.
- Plan and organise work within deadlines.

KNOWLEDGE
- Information sources (e.g. timetables, directories, hotel guides, car hire, maps, exchange rates).
- Services offered by booking agents.
- Details of engagements to be made (e.g. who, when, where and how).
- Booking procedures and allowances used in organisations.
- Telephone procedures and techniques.

- Overseas requirements: visas/vaccinations etc.

The possible assessment methods for these elements of competence could be: observation in the workplace; discussion with the student; the production of evidence (written/typed messages, letters of confirmation etc.) or simulation. None of these methods would be disabling for a visually-impaired student.

Advice, equipment and training are available from a number of public sources such as the PACTs operated by the Department of Employment free of charge (other employment services such as a free reader service are available from the same source); charitable sources such as the Royal National Institute for the Blind and educational and training establishments as outlined elsewhere in this volume. However, none of these adaptations will detract from the efficacy of the student in the workplace.

To recapitulate our route:

- identify the national standards;
- access awards (NVQ);
- carry out analysis of underpinning skills and knowledge;
- design competence based training;
- establish strategy for assessment (optimising validity, reliability, sufficient and cost effectiveness);
- ensure the quality of assessment (by having qualified assessors);
- identify the individual needs of the student;
- identify and provide the equipment and a suitable environment for delivery and assessment;
- identify and establish a network of placement providers to give access to students in order to demonstrate competence in a realistic working environment;
- establish a procedure for workplace providers to gain assessment qualifications;
- provide opportunities for simulated performance;
- carry out training and assessment;
- submit for certification.

Conclusion

As we begin to understand competence and how we achieve it, we see almost immediately the benefits it may have for a visually-impaired student. If the training is designed to facilitate learning and enable the student to demonstrate competence (not to imply it), then we are not only recognising but accepting that competence is available to all whether they have a visual impairment or not.

Therefore a better definition of COMPETENCE could be:

Career opportunities
Opportunities that are equal
Mobility of employment for its owner
Potential recognition
Equal access
Training designed for the individual
Easy access
Non-discrimination
Certificate of achievement
Enlightenment for all its users.

References

Burke, J.W. (ed) (1990) *Competency Based Education and Training* (Falmer Press, London).

Fletcher, S. (1991) *NVQs: Standards and Competence* (Kogan Page, London).

Jessop, G. (1991) *Outcomes: NVQs and the Emerging Model of Education and Training* (Falmer Press, London).

National Council for Vocational Qualifications (1988a) *Introducing a National System of Credit Accumulation* (NCVQ London).

National Council for Vocational Qualifications (1988b) *The NCVQ Criteria and Related Guidelines* (NCVQ London).

National Council for Vocational Qualifications (1988c) *Implementation Note 4. Assessment in National Vocational Qualifications* (NCVQ London).

National Council for Vocational Qualifications (1990) *Research and Development Report No. 5. Emerging issues in the Utilisation of NVQs* (NCVQ London).

CHAPTER SEVEN

Assessment for Adults who are Visually Impaired

Bernadette Caffrey

Background

Established in 1949, the Rehabilitation Institute now stands as the largest existing vocational training service in Ireland. Currently, it offers training to over 2000 adults who are disabled and operates 43 centres nationally. Originally, it was designed as a response to those suffering from tuberculosis during the post-war period but through its continuous development it has emerged as a system which offers a more integrative approach. Almost unique in design, the Rehabilitation Institute caters for the needs of those people who present with a broad range of disabilities where a multi-dimensional perspective is adopted. Such an approach immediately removes one from a typecast unilateral construction of disability in terms of a single label. The latter at once confines dimensions and will be discussed in more detail below.

Given the above, the development of a coherent assessment procedure is necessary. Such has evolved inside the development of Roslyn College National Training Centre since its foundation in 1983. The college was established in order to forward the opportunity for those adults who are disabled yet have the potential to train within areas such as architectural draughting, graphic design, electronics, business organisation photography, computer programming, secretarial book keeping, pre-university course, professional cookery and academic foundation courses. Of particular interest is the development of an assessment procedure designed for those with various degrees of visual impairment. In this chapter, particular attention will be given to the construction of this assessment system and how it may be adapted in a useful and meaningful way. Our main focus of interest is specific in terms of assessment techniques developed for those who are non-sighted and non-braille users (referred to throughout this chapter as Group B). Accordingly an outline of criteria-referenced assessment adaptations, assessment profiles, and results will be presented and discussed.

Criteria-referenced assessment

More traditional methods of assessment have tended to adopt a predictive model which often assumes homogeneity of group and at once ignores non-impartiality due to cultural bias. In an attempt to progress towards a wider focus, given the broad range of people who are disabled within the College, a criterion-referenced form of assessment has been adopted. As alluded to above, in order to consider each individual outside any single label or distinct category it is necessary to construe any given disability along a multi-dimensional perspective upon which clients' needs can be addressed over several areas, namely: cognitive, vocational, environmental, educational, medical, psychomotor and psychosocial. Given the transactional effect of environmental issues upon vocational training or indeed any combination of these dimensions, it is conceived as being more useful to assess the client in terms of strengths and weaknesses, as opposed to the latter alone. On the contrary, criterion-referenced tests are designed so as to facilitate such a process during initial assessment and indeed within continuous planning of vocational training.

The assessment procedure as such is in three separate but interlinked stages. Clients are assessed within a group setting initially and then interviewed individually. The interview is structured in such a way as to gather information around the client's views of assessment and expectations together with their vocational, medical, social and educational history. The group assessment investigates each client's general language usage ability and learning potential using the Mill Hill Vocabulary Scale and Ravens Progressive Matrices respectively. Additionally, a measure of the percentage of educational standard achieved over that which is required for each course is readily available from results of the criterion-referenced tests which are based on course demands analysis. Tests currently in use for this purpose include the Drumcondea Mathematics and English Comprehension Exercise. A

Differential Aptitude Test for Spelling can also be administered.

The second stage of assessment provides an opportunity for the client to complete course samples within close simulation of the real training environment. Performance is measured against necessary standards of motivation, manual dexterity, accuracy, speed, understanding of oral instructions and educational levels required alongside environmental adaptation needed. Clients carry out self-assessment along similar areas. This allows comparison of results and inherently measures levels of clients' anticipation and the degree to which they are realistic about their vocational goals. Given the nature of the assessment each instructor is immediately equipped to observe how each client manages with the psychosocial demands of the given task – and throughout provides the means to highlight areas which are apparent strengths and those areas which will need to be addressed. Comparing instructors' and clients' assessment may form a platform from which goals and objectives may be discussed and negotiated. It has been found that the degree to which each client's self-assessment is consistent or inconsistent with that of the instructors is a good indicator as to what degree the clients will need to effect change in their life in order to successfully respond to training. These plans and aspirations are discussed at length in a one-to-one interview following completion of course samples. Against the background of the client's own personal history and job research (which they have been asked to submit as a pre-requisite for a stage two assessment) together with results thus far, an informed decision is made as to whether or not any of the courses present as potentially suitable training options for the client.

The third stage of assessment is structured in such a way as to facilitate those clients who have proven successful over both the stage one and stage two assessment, by means of a six week trial period. The client is given the opportunity to meet up with one of the assessment team members to review progress to date and identify possible support or intervention where required – especially with regard to medication, social life, home environment and training issues. The client also meets with the course instructor during this period in order to identify and negotiate actions which need to be carried out more specifically with regard to the technical aspects of teaching. Development and progress of each client is systematically monitored and the client is encouraged to take on a leading role in this.

In reviewing current developments with regard to assessment

design for those adults who are visually impaired, greater emphasis is placed on adaptations to stage one and two assessment given their more immediate relevance compared with the stage three confirmatory period.

Group profile

A group profile of 46 clients, 37 of whom have since completed courses, five of whom are currently attending the college and four of whom have recently completed assessment is presented below in terms of the following: degree to which they are visually impaired; age range; level of cognitive functioning and vocational interest, together with information on course attended, where appropriate. All assessments were carried out between 1987 and 1992.

Those clients who were partially visually impaired constituted 73.92% of the total number assessed while the remainder were diagnosed as those who were non-sighted except for perception of shades of light and darkness. Upon further analysis, it was revealed that 78.3% of cases which were studied were congenital in etiology while 21.97 % were acquired in nature. A detailed overview of impairment type is presented in Table 7.1.

Age ranged between eighteen years and 46 years with mean age falling at 25 years; this approximately reflects the age range of clients currently attending the college. Generally, most clients were of average or above average intelligence; more specific details in terms of results yielded from the Ravens Progessive Matrices and General Language Usage ability will be presented below under the heading 'Results'.

TABLE 7.1 Percentage and type of visual impairment

N = 46

Visual impairment type	% Population
Congenital cataract	21.73
Diabetics retinopathy	8.69
Nystagmus (albinism)	8.69
VI following surgical intervention	2.17
Macula aplasia	2.17
Retinitis pigmentosa	8.69
Glaucoma and congenital cataracts	4.34
R.T.A. optic nerve damage light perception only	26.08

R.T.A. detached retina (RE)	2.17
Bilateral keratoconus	2.17
Bilateral retinal dystrophy	10.93
R.T.A optic nerve damage light perception L.E.	2.17

Besides those clients who have completed assessment of late, 28% attended a twelve week telephone course; 12% attended the secretarial course; 14% attended the business studies course; 9% attended the pre-univsersity course; 2% attended the electronics course while 35% attended the computer programming course.

Methodology and adaptations to assessment

Given the various degrees to which the impairment affected the ability to participate, certain adaptations to the procedural methodology were necessary in order to facilitate this group, particularly those who were significantly visually impaired. Those who were partially sighted, unable to read standard print and not competent in using braille (Group B) were facilitated by provision of magnifying print using a closed-circuit television or simply enlarging the standard print. These constituted 47.6% of the group. The percentage of clients competent in using braille amounted to over a quarter of those assessed while 23.8% coped well with standard print when wearing corrective lenses.

Assessment for those presented as being totally non-sighted except for light perception and not competent in using braille necessitated a specialised form of assessment which is indeed still in its developmental stages. The following is a detailed outline of adaptations made to stage one and stage two assessment for this group.

Adaptations to stage one assessment for Group B

All candidates were the victims of road traffic accidents occurring over the last nine years. Given the nature of their disability and limited if not sparse knowledge in using braille, tests were administered using audiotapes. These included the Mill Hill Vocabulary Scale, the Differential Aptitude Test (DAT) for spelling and the Drumcondra Criterion Referenced Mathematics Test. As the Ravens Progressive Matrices was not conducive to this form of presentation, non-verbal logical reasoning scores were not attainable. Similarly, the Criterion-Referenced English Comprehension Cloze

Test was not used given its inherent cognitive demands if presented on tape. It was decided that results yielded from this test would at most give an unreliable indication of the client's memory recall and hence be rendered invalid as a measure of one's ability in terms of English comprehension.

In relation to the absence of information with regard to learning potential, as may be inferred from the Ravens Progressive Matrices Results, it may be assumed that all candidates were of average intelligence. This assumption is based on the type and level of educational and employment history – together with results yielded from those tests referred to above, in particular scores attained on the Mill Hill Vocabulary Scale. It is worthwhile noting that traditional methods of assessment for general intelligence have tended to use the verbal section of the Weschler Adult Intelligence Scale as a means to extrapolate a score of intelligence quotient. However, for reasons discussed earlier surrounding norm-referenced testing and in view of the fact that tests administered during this assessment were relatively quite high in verbal content in comparison to our usual assessment process, its usefulness for the client on this occasion was strongly questioned.

Procedure

The assessment process was scheduled over a three day period. Clients attended an initial induction period where they became more familiar with using tapes and dictaphones. Throughout induction, clients were encouraged to use the dictaphone as a memory bank, particularly in relation to sample mathematical problems presented. Induction was systematically structured so as to include repeated demonstration and practice in order to decrease the number of potential extraneous variables. Clients were also encouraged to record any difficulties experienced in order that the process itself could be qualitatively evaluated. As described earlier, each client was interviewed on a one-to-one basis in partial fulfilment of assessment.

Adaptations to stage two assessment

The stage two assessment is designed to include a three part computer programme aptitude battery, quiz test, practical exercises and demonstrations. Usually, it is scheduled over one or one and half days.

Briefly, the logical diagrams which form one part of the computer programme aptitude battery present problems expressed in English with schematic diagrams in the form of flow charts. The client is expected to solve the given problem constructively using the flow charts to meet certain conditions. Given that the test relies heavily on visual presentation, by its nature, it is not suitable for use as an assessment tool when working with adults who have a severe visual impairment.

A similar induction period to stage one assessment features as part of the programme for stage two assessment. Following this, in order to allay the clients' fears and anxiety related to testing, a letter series exercise, which forms one part of the Computer Programme Aptitude Battery (CPAB), is administered on audiotape. The client is required to complete the pattern to the letter series presented. Test duration is usually ten minutes and it includes 26 questions in all.

In comparison to the logical diagrams, the CPAB reasoning exercise in use proved to be readily amenable to testing procedures as described above under adaptations to stage one assessment. In this test, problems are presented in English and the client is expected to reduce the problem to a mathematical format. Test duration is usually 20 minutes.

In the quiz test, which is a problem-solving exercise, an arrangement of numbers is presented in boxes and the client is required to construct a series of instructions adhering to certain conditions in order to achieve a specific final arrangement. Procedural methods are once again similar to those outlined under stage one assessment.

Upon completion of the test, the client is asked to carry out a number of relatively simple practical exercises for a period of up to 30 minutes following demonstration and instruction. Finally, the client is invited to spend some time with current students where he or she is given some demonstration of course projects completed.

Unlike the usual stage two assessment procedure, this specialised assessment is somewhat extended. Small discussion groups form a large feature of its design, in order to help clients feel at ease and encourage them to absorb the information presented. In addition to this, the client is also invited to attend two interviews, one carried out by the instructor with regard to technical and vocational interest, while the second interview is conducted by a member of the assessment team in order to feed back results. It is important to note that the assessment process is intentionally punctuated with various elements in order to facilitate the high levels of concentration required.

Stage one results

Results yielded from the Ravens Progressive Matrices would suggest that for the majority (nearly 80% of those assessed) their scores would fall within the average range of ability. It would appear that while 17% of the population tested on the Ravens Progressive Matrices scored above average, only 3% of subjects scored below average in terms of learning potential. As mentioned earlier, scores pertaining to learning potential were not attainable for almost 7% of the clients and may only be assumed to be close to average ability as extrapolated from scores on verbal ability tests as detailed below.

Using the Mill Hill Vocabulary Scale, results obtained were as follows: 89% of the group would appear to be verbally average while the remaining 11% are slightly below average in terms of verbal ability. These results include those who attended for the specialised assessment. In relation to the educational requirements necessary to cope with the academic demands of the course, 87% of scores achieved on the Criterion Referenced Drumcondra Mathematics and English Comprehension were well within percentage of course requirements. Subsequently, of those who are currently attending the College or who have since been discharged, only 13% needed to attend the Educational Foundation course prior to being accepted on the technical training courses.

Reviewing educational results for those candidates who were administered tests using audiotapes, it has been revealed that the majority of these clients scored quite close to criteria levels except for one candidate whose scores were inconsistently low given his educational standard. However, these results would need to be qualified by the fact that inherent cognitive demands were made by the very nature of the assessment itself. With regard to methods used, client feedback would suggest that while initial stages of the induction period presented as quite demanding, most expressed satisfaction once they were familiar with equipment. This would certainly be supported by overall results and observation where it was noticed that people worked more independently over time and queries decreased.

Stage Two Results

It would be expected that the majority of those who attended for this specialised assessment would indeed attend for two specific modules of training given their performance over stage one and stage two assessment. The section following is a brief outline of those modules which have been designed in order to enable the potential candidates to equip themselves with those skills necessary to cope with the demands of word processing and more advanced computer commands. It was concluded that they would more appropriately match the candidate's vocational goals as opposed to computer programming.

Module 1

This may be divided into two parts: familiarisation with specialised equipment; and basic computer demands. Depending upon current knowledge and experience candidates will be trained to use a speech synthesiser as a means to familiarise themselves with basic computer concepts. For those clients who present with limited knowledge of braille, an introduction to the use of Perkins brailler, scanner and braille embosser will be given – clients will be encouraged and supported in increasing skills with regard to braille usage.

Module 2

The second module has been structured to involve teaching within word processing *Word Star* and *Word Perfect*. Upon successful completion of these areas clients will hopefully progress on to more advanced training in computer commands.

Overall results for those who have completed courses to date

Out of the total group of 46, to date, 37 students have completed courses. The total number of those placed would approximate to 62% which closely reflects the college placement rate in general. A course and percentage breakdown is tabulated below (Table 7.2). Over 43% of those placed were given the opportunity to join the open employment market while just less than 20% progressed to higher level training or education, in most cases third level education. It must also be noted that 35% who sucessfully completed courses were not immediately placed. A little less than 3% left voluntarily prior to course completion but were transferred to training at a lower level than that offered in Roslyn College.

Table 7.2 Numbers of students (i) completing the course (ii) placed in emloyment

Course	Completed Course	Placed	%
Telephone	9	2	22
Business Studies	5	5	100
P.U.C.	4	4	100
Secretarial	5	2	40
Electronics	1	1	100
Programming	13	9	69

Conclusion

Reviewing these assessment and training results it would appear that an assessment process which utilises criterion-referenced as opposed to norm-referenced testing and advocates a self-assessment system is qualitatively speaking most valuable. This is immediately evident upon close examination of percentage placement rates achieved. Equally, the importance of designing a constructive 'user friendly' method of assessment for those presenting with visual impairments to the degree where light alone is perceived and whose use of braille is non existent is also evident. However, there are a number of aspects which have emerged throughout its development which will need to be further investigated. Analysis of placement figures and percentages of those clients not immediately placed gives support to the concept of a loop-back system. This would make it possible to monitor students' progress and quality of existing placements together with success rates of those not immediately placed upon course completion. Upon examination of the assessment procedure adapted for those with additional difficulties, it may be concluded that in terms of its overall structured design and effectiveness, a coherent induction period must be said to be of paramount importance where intial one-to-one support is essential. As mentioned earlier, tests for achievement standards for English comprehension in relation to course requirements were not used due to their apparent cognitive demands inside this form of assessment. A similar test will need to be developed devoid of such demands. Simultaneously, extraneous cognitive demands akin to the

Drumcondra Mathematics Test will also need to be qualified and recorded. Nonetheless, it should be emphasised that, while the system will need to be more finely attuned in order to narrow these gaps, it furnishes some useful information especially in terms of the clients' ability to adapt and work independently.

It also emerged that a flexible modular system is necessary in order to design course content and structure around the client's needs, as evidenced within this group. Following completion of these modules, review and evaluation will need to be carried out in order to assess its design and overall objective against placement rate.

Finally, amidst assessment design the value of a client-directed approach has been once again realised throughout its development. Its value cannot be over-estimated in terms of working proactively on issues which may arise early on in the initial assessment period and indeed in its contribution to creating quality vocational training.

References

Drumcondra Criteria Referenced Mathematics Test (1977) (Dublin: Educational Research Centre).

Palormo, J.M. (1964) *Computer Aptitude Battery* (Science Research Associates, Inc.).

Popham, W.J. (1978) *Criterion Referenced Measurement* (NJ: Prentice Hall).

Ravens, J. C. (1979) *Mill Hill Vocabulary Scale* (London: H. K. Lewis).

Ravens, J. C. (1979) *Standard Progressive Matrices* (London: H. K. Lewis).

Roslyn Park Comprehension Test Assessment Unit, The National Training College, Rehabilitation Institute (unpublished)

Roslyn Park National Training College Assessment Unit Description (unpublished)

CHAPTER EIGHT

Counselling the Visually-impaired Adult

Maggie Rowe

Counselling is an area which is becoming increasingly recognised as a vital aspect of further education provision. This chapter looks at the role of the professional counsellor in helping the adult client group to come to terms with visual impairment and the problems that they are likely to face in further education.

Many people use the word 'counselling' to describe an activity they embark upon with others. It is sometimes difficult to recognise the activity which occupies my working practice when I hear others' definitions implicit in how they talk about counselling. Sometimes their intervention would be better described as advice or guidance, sometimes even as social control. I intend to describe my working model of counselling and use this definition throughout this chapter.

In their Invitation to Membership (1977) the British Association for Counselling, the body which nationally represents counselling in Britain, defines 'counselling' as:

> when a person, occupying regularly or temporarily the role of counsellor, offers and agrees explicitly to give time, attention and respect to another person, or persons, who will be temporarily in the role of client. The task of counselling is to give the client an opportunity to explore, discover and clarify ways of living more resourcefully and towards greater well-being. The counsellor provides a secure and facilitating atmosphere for this to occur.

In this model, which is essentially person-centred, counselling is a relationship aimed at facilitating the process of self-determination with the client; it is non-hierarchical.

By person-centred, I mean that the client is the focus of the relationship and makes the choices about change. I do not, as a counsellor, offer solutions; I offer a relationship where my client can feel safe enough to explore their personal difficulties and move towards change; a relationship in which my client is enabled to recognise and use their own personal resources more effectively. By non-hierarchical I mean that both of us engaged in this relationship have skills and wisdom that will be used co-operatively in the counselling process. My emphasis in this model of counselling is on the relationship between my client and myself and the facilitating nature of this relationship.

For my counselling to be effective I must demonstrate the essential qualities of genuineness, non-possessive warmth and empathy and I must treat my client with non-judgmental respect. It is essential not to attempt to impose my agenda or my pace on my client. My task is to facilitate self-empowerment and I cannot do this if I want what I want for my client on the basis of my own experience, my own judgements and even my own prejudices.

Dr Carl Rogers, the American psychologist and founder of person-centred counselling, expressed the central tenet of this way of being with a client with clarity when he wrote: 'the individual has within himself vast resources for self-understanding, for altering his self-concept, his attitudes, and his self-directed behaviour – and (that) these resources can be tapped if only a definable climate of facilitative psychological attitudes can be provided' (Rogers 1974). This, then, is how I define the counselling I strive to practice and the definition I will use throughout this chapter.

My task here is to look at the role of the professional counsellor in working with a client group defined in two ways – adult and visually-impaired. Whilst I will progress to considerations of my work with adults who happen to have a visual impairment, I want to clarify a point which is central to the way I approach my work with individuals.

For reasons which will become clear I will give you a brief description of myself. I am a woman, rapidly approaching the age of 50, the mother of two children who are now young women, I wear glasses because I am short-sighted; I am rather overweight. All of these characteristics are parts of who I am, and of course there are many other parts of me that I could use to define myself but which I have no wish to share with you at this moment! But if I only define myself by my age, or my weight, for example, I arrive at a totally unbalanced view of myself and lose sight of my wholeness. Therefore I disable myself.

For the clients with whom I work, their age and their visual impairment are only parts of who they are, parts which may have an effect on their self-image, but which are, nevertheless, only parts of their whole being. In this writing, as in my work with clients, I want to keep this very firmly in mind. When I 'see' only a visual impairment I lose my focus on the individuality of those seeking my help, and thereby collude with the discrimination of a society that limits an individual by their disability.

I work no differently with a young adult with a visual impairment than I would with a young adult who has freckles. I listen to that individual and leave them to clarify for me the source of their emotional ill-health. The source may be linked to the visual impairment or the freckles, or it may not, and it is important that I do not bring my assumptions about what having a visual impairment or freckles may mean to my relationship with this person. For one person whose self-concept is good and strong, having a visual impairment will not limit their feelings of self-worth, for another, whose self-concept is poor, having freckles may be a devastating and totally disabling characteristic.

If, however, we are to look in this chapter at the value of counselling for adults who have a visual impairment, some examination of the implications for psychological health of a visual impairment is necessary.

The first distinction I want to make is between young adults who are congenitally visually impaired, whose impairment has been with them since birth, and those who have had sight and become blind as a result of an accident or another medical condition that affects their sight e.g. brain tumour, stroke, diabetes etc.

The first group, the congenitally blind, are on the whole primarily psychologically disabled by external factors: society's attitudes, parental fear and over-protectiveness, parental rejection, the attitudes of the 'caring' professions, a lack of appropriate resources and learning materials and experiences for their personal development. There are many young adults who fall into this category who lead emotionally healthy, integrated lives. They have been lucky enough to have had good life experiences, they have been allowed to take risks, allowed to learn by making mistakes, treated with respect for their individuality by the professionals who surround them, trusted to find their own place in the world and offered appropriate learning resources to do that. The message they have been given about themselves by all these influences is that they are valued individuals.

Others are less fortunate. They may have been surrounded from birth by attitudes which give them messages that say 'you are not to be trusted', 'you cannot do things for yourself', 'you need to be protected from your own curiosity, your natural instinct to explore your world, both physically and emotionally'. For these young people the move to a more independent learning environment at sixteen can be a traumatic, confusing and potentially disturbing time. The second group, the adventitiously blind, can also be disabled by these external attitudes to their new condition but where this happens it seems to be confirmation of the internal dislocation that occurs with sudden loss of sight. The loss of confidence and of self-esteem that occurs when the primary means of making sense of ourselves in relation to our environment and other people within it is lost, is immensely disabling. 'How do I know how other people in the room feel about me when I can no longer rely on the visual clues I have always used?' 'Am I still loveable, able to love?' 'How do I know where the dangers are?' 'Can I take care of myself any more?' This fundamental trauma of sudden loss of sight is immensely disturbing to an individual's sense of self-worth. Often it is precisely at this time that professionals and family are urging the acquisition of new skills in mobility, communication and living in an attempt to 'make it better'. In my experience it is not until such a person has been able to explore the depths of their despair at their new condition and has found a companion who is able to communicate his or her understanding of this desolate and lonely place they find themselves in, and who is willing to stay with them for as long as they need to find their worth again, that new skills teaching is ever effective. These, then, are elements that we need to bear in mind when offering therapeutic relationships to adults in FE who are visually impaired. But I cannot stress enough how important it is to let each individual tell us for themselves what is the source of their disease. If I assume that the student I am working with is withdrawn and depressed because of her visual impairment, I close my mind to any other source of her distress. I may never create a safe enough place for her to disclose that she has been sexually abused in childhood, for example. If I assume that the grief exhibited by a client belongs only to his loss of sight, I may miss the opportunity for him to heal from the loss of his relationship with his girlfriend.

Many of the issues that I work with are those I would expect to find amongst a sighted peer group. There is often an overlay of damage to the self-concept because of a visual impairment and society's attitudes to that, but it is rarely the primary cause of the unhappiness and lack of well-being felt by the client.

Let us look at the second of the ways in which the people we work with are defined, that is by the educational setting of further education. What are the implications for an individual in this? Some students will arrive at FE college straight from school. Like their sighted peers, visually-impaired young adults can find this transition a difficult and traumatic time. It is another step along the road to adulthood and independence, another step away from home. The more adult environment of a place of learning where the individual is required to take more responsibility for their own learning, to be self-disciplined and more self-directed in their learning and their social pursuits than at school, can be a challenging and confusing place. Even young people who have had the opportunity to find themselves and feel good about themselves in a school environment can find the transition to college disturbing for a while until they find their feet. For those who have been in a very sheltered school or family environment this can be an overwhelming experience.

Alongside this difficult transition in the external environment is the more fraught internal transition from childhood to adulthood with all its insecurities and fears, its curiosities and the need to explore boundaries that are changing. Cast your mind back to how you felt when you were sixteen. Can you remember how difficult a time that was for you? Were you gripped by the desperation of wanting to be an adult and yet terrified of what that meant? Did you need to feel like others in your group? Were you excited by and at the same time fearful of the way your body was responding? Try to imagine meeting these situations without ever having had access to the information most of us have through books, magazines, films as well as our day-to-day information gathering through visual cues that help us to make sense of ourselves in the world. For the young person who has been sheltered, prevented by concern from self-exploration and exploring the world, how much more terrifying must this transition be? Some have been taken care of in such a stifling way that they exhibit a 'learned helplessness' and wait placidly to be told what to do and how to do it. Others defend themselves against their fear and anxiety with an outwardly aggressive behaviour which belies their panic and their vulnerability.

Other students arrive in further education at a more mature age to retrain in vocational skills, sometimes after losing sight, sometimes after long and debilitating periods of unemployment. This transition can be as difficult for them. Often they have very high expectations of what a college course has to offer them, and when the reality does not match their hopes, many do not have the assertiveness skills necessary to ask for their needs to be met in a way which can be heard and responded to by the training providers. Their appropriate anger inappropriately expressed is branded as 'difficult' and 'obstructive' and the vicious downward spiral of helplessness and self-loathing and consequently even less appropriate behaviour continues. It is extremely difficult, if not impossible, to be assertive when you feel yourself to be worthless.

What counselling has to offer adults who, for whatever reason, feel worthless and who have lost, or never had, any positive self-image, is a relationship in which they can begin to feel valued, accepted, understood; a relationship in which they can trust the helping professional to be consistently available to them, allowing them the time they need to explore the parts of themselves that are hurting and confused; a relationship in which the counsellor really believes that this person has within them the capacity to grow towards their own unique fulfilment and rejects the pursuit of control or authority over them. If the relationship the client experiences is healthy and avoids the danger of relating only to a fragment of them and their experience, but rather holds the whole person in esteem, then inevitably the negative self-concept which has grown thanks to the condemnation and criticism of others can begin to change. Perhaps it would be helpful to illustrate my theorising with two brief case histories. For reasons of confidentiality, an essential prerequisite of a counselling relationship, names and identifying details are changed, but the descriptions of the process of the clients' journeys within the therapeutic relationship are accurate.

Graham

Graham referred himself to counselling within a few weeks of starting his college course. He is congenitally blind, in his mid-thirties with additional physical handicaps. He had come to college to retrain on a vocational course where manual dexterity was important.

In our first session, after negotiating our boundaries of time, length of contract, confidentiality, etc., Graham poured out his reasons for coming to see me. He was overwhelmed with a feeling of 'not coping'. In the six months prior to his coming to college his wife had returned to her home in Australia and Graham's fear was that there would be no place for him there with her when his course ended in 18 months time. He felt undermined by his parents whose home he had returned to on his wife's departure. His self-esteem was very low and he avoided the tears he was close to throughout the session by using sarcastic throwaway remarks about himself.

As the relationship progressed Graham disclosed more and more about the source of his despair. He felt different, isolated, alone. One attitude which really insulted him was that he was never seen as a 'threat' in terms of his sexuality; he felt his masculinity was being ignored, unvalued and unaccepted. Another was the message he was receiving from college about the amount of independence he 'should' be capable of, but at this moment felt unable to cope with.

There were many times with Graham when I would have found it very easy to reassure him or try to rescue him from the enormous pain he was feeling. If I had done that I would have been guilty of behaving in the way he felt others behaved towards him which left him feeling unvalued and without rights and power. If I had tried to 'make it better' either by doing things for him or by suggesting ways he might behave in order to elicit the response he wanted from others, I would not have been valuing and hearing the part of him that was hurting so much.

Graham and I stayed with this part of him for several sessions during which he graphically described his feeling of grief and allowed it a voice. His loss was of 'normality' and 'opportunity'. He felt that his blindness and physical handicap had left him with the loss of 'normal' manhood as a sexual being. He recognised that he had learned 'other devices' to keep people interested in him, notably his quick wit and his sense of humour, but beneath that he was crying out to be wanted and recognised as a man. He often smiled and laughed when he talked about his pain, particularly in relation to his feelings of self-worth.

After ten sessions Graham was beginning to find his own insights into his behaviour in our relationship and to make links with how he was outside the sessions. He realised that 'burying the pain because it hurts too much to get it out and look at it' was ineffective because he felt permanently disabled by it. This awareness gave him the courage to take the next step – to give voice to his pain. He spent much of the next few sessions sobbing, held in the grip of deepest despair. He found it hard to leave this behind in between sessions and his college work suffered consequently.

It was after this that he recognised that the course he was

following was not the right one for him. He was struggling in many ways, although it took him some time to come to the decision to change courses.

Graham found that having been able to voice his despair he began to find feelings of anger. I felt heartened by this because I recognise anger as a healthy emotion which can be the backbone of healing. He was angry about his abandonment by his wife, began to acknowledge that their relationship was one in which he had always felt too dependent and decided to file for a divorce.

From time to time Graham stepped back into his desperate sense of separateness and isolation but more and more he was able to be with his anger. Often it was anger with me because our session had to end. But gradually he became less disorientated, physically and emotionally. He began to discover a sense of well-being socially and he no longer felt an outcast in our microcosmic society at college. Graham began to be accepting of his feelings; he became more aware of his own behaviour in assuming victimisation and began to change that behaviour. He used less negative, undermining talk about himself and began to recognise where he put himself at the mercy of others and used that awareness to change the unhealthy patterns of behaviour he had used throughout his life.

By the end of our relationship Graham was able to spontaneously recognise his feelings of sadness at our ending and give them full and healthy expression. He had formed a relationship with a woman of his own age that he thought had the possibility of a future, where he felt valued for his sexuality and for who he was. He left college to live independently for the first time in his life. He felt able to cope.

Three years later I still get an occasional phone call from Graham. He still lives independently. His relationship continues to flourish. He has a fulfilling social life. Unfortunately he, like many others at this time of recession, cannot find employment, but his growing sense of self-worth is not diminished by that.

I am sure that the key for Graham in our work together was that I was able to communicate to him my trust that he would find his own way through to his own healing. If I had wavered in that trust I would have confirmed his worst fears about himself – that he was so worthless and so helpless in his own life that I, the professional knew better than he. My willingness to be intimate with the parts of himself he felt so badly about and not to defend myself against them, but to accept them and stay with them, helped him to become intimate with himself and his wholeness and to become accepting and valuing of himself. Our therapeutic relationship lasted two years.

Jill

Jill is seventeen. She came to college straight from a residential school where she stayed during the week but travelled home for weekends. She is partially-sighted. She asked for time with me a few weeks after starting college because she had 'a big problem'.

During our first session Jill was very distressed. She was able to articulate the source of her distress very clearly: she had received a letter from her mother which had left her feeling very uncomfortable. Before coming to college her mother had made her promise that she would discontinue the close and loving relationship she had established with a young man at school, who was also transferring to college at the same time as Jill.

Jill's mother was clearly behaving in a very protective way. The letter contained the suggestion that now Jill had finished with B she and her mother would return to the close, loving relationship they had before B came into Jill's life. Jill's discomfort was that, although she had promised her mother during the holidays that she would finish with him, when she met B again as the college term started she realised that their relationship was really important to her. She knew that she wanted to continue it, indeed had been continuing it, and now felt very upset to be deceiving her mother. This was compounded by the fear that her mother would either take her away from college if she told her the truth – an action that had been threatened when the break-up had been demanded at home, or that she should be rejected at home and would not be welcome there again.

Jill clearly loved both her mother and B. As we explored her situation she was able to recognise that her mother was asking her to make a choice she was not prepared to make. She began to find some anger about that and give it a voice in the sessions. She wanted both mother and B and felt angry at her mother's lack of trust in her. Clearly Jill felt stuck and powerless, but as we explored her powerlessness she began to recognise that she was giving her power away to her mother. Mother has always made all the decisions for Jill in her life and here was a decision she wanted to take responsibility for herself. We explored her fears and she came to the realisation that her mother could not force her to leave college if she didn't want to and if she was rejected at home she would feel an enormous loss, but she could survive that. She felt welcome in B's home, so a roof over her head during holidays was ensured.

This seemed to free Jill to be able to decide to 'speak' to her mother in a more adult way than she ever had before. She decided to write to her as her experience of speaking directly in the past had resulted in mother 'ranting and raving and crying' at her and she felt unable to communicate clearly and always gave in to the emotional manipulation.

In her letter Jill spoke very clearly of her love for her mother as well as for B and her recognition that mother was forcing her to make a choice that was not of her making. She was clear that if she was forced, she would choose B and that she wanted mother to begin to let her go, to help her to take steps into adulthood and that she wanted her support with that, but if that were not possible, she would do it alone.

Jill asked for further sessions to carry her over the time when mother would respond to the letter.

Jill was clearly surprised by her mother's response. After threatening to come to college to 'sort it out', her mother was able to accept Jill's growing ability to take responsibility for her own decisions, including her right to make mistakes and learn from them. She has not been thrown out of the family home, indeed Jill and her mother seem to have been able to take the steps towards a more adult relationship.

It would have been easy for me to bombard Jill with an 'understanding' of how her mother must feel in this situation. To do that would have undermined Jill's growing ability to take care of herself and her own needs rather than to act from a position of taking care of her mother's needs as she had done in the past. Our relationship lasted six sessions.

In conclusion, I would emphasise again that the professional counsellor working in an FE setting with the visually impaired will work no differently than he or she would with any other client group. The difficulties of the transition to further education and the overlay of others' attitudes to a visual impairment are simply two variables which may or may not be relevant to an individual client. Of paramount importance is an attitude of respect for the uniqueness of each individual and their own experience and the fundamental belief that they can, given the right therapeutic conditions, find their own path to emotional well-being. Many clients come to counselling looking for yet another 'expert' to tell them what to do, despite the damage they have already received at the hands of those who have tried to direct their lives for them. To fulfil such a role, the counsellor would deny the possibility of encouraging a relationship where the client can begin to tentatively experience the beginnings of self-acceptance and change their fundamental belief about their own worth. Perhaps the disabled, including those with a visual impairment, need these conditions more urgently because of the way society feels free to deny such groups their autonomy and their individual uniqueness and potential. Let us not fall into that trap.

References

British Association for Counselling (1977) *Invitation to membership* BAC: (Rugby).

Rogers, C. R. (1974) 'In retrospect: forty six years', *American Psychologist*, 29.

CHAPTER NINE

Communication – Options and Issues

Stephen McCall

The way that people with visual impairments gain access to, store and pass on information to others varies according to individual circumstances and will be influenced by factors such as age, ability, the nature of their visual impairment and the presence or absence of additional disabilities. Their methods of communicating will also be determined by the purpose and nature of the task in hand, the training and support they receive and the materials and equipment available.

This chapter will address itself primarily to the needs of people with visual impairments in the 18-60 age group who are in education, rehabilitation, in paid employment or (like 83% of the registered blind who live at home) unemployed. The main print and print substitute communication media available will be considered and their advantages and disadvantages will be explored.

Heinze (1986) describes communication as a two way process involving 'receptive' modes such as listening and reading and 'expressive' modes such as writing and typing. The receptive modes for people with visual impairments will include reading through print or print substitutes such as braille and Moon, and listening through tapes or synthetic speech. The expressive modes will encompass writing in braille, typing and handwriting.

Reading

Normal print can be a primary medium of communication for a significant proportion of the severely visually impaired in further education provided appropriate assistance in the form of magnification or enlargement is available.

Magnification

Although the term Low Vision Aids (LVAs) is sometimes taken to include spectacles, the term is most commonly applied to the variety of magnifying devices designed specifically for the low vision user. These aids vary in power, sophistication and price; some are designed to improve distance vision while others are specifically for near vision tasks such as reading. LVAs for close work include hand-held or stand-mounted magnifiers which may contain built-in illumination allowing the user to read very close to the page while retaining adequate illumination. Specialist aids also include powerful spectacle mounted magnifiers which have the advantage of freeing the hands for writing or typing.

A difficulty that arises for the student who needs to access large amounts of written material is that the more powerful LVAs such as spectacle mounted lenses require working distances close to the reading materials. Users may experience fatigue (Corn 1986) during extended periods of study.

Closed Circuit Television magnifiers (CCTVs) can obviate some of the problems of fatigue. They offer on-screen magnification of up to 60 times in monochrome or colour allowing users with even the smallest amounts of functional vision access to text or diagrams. The degree of magnification and the levels of contrast that can be achieved allow the reader to view the screen from a comfortable working distance. CCTVs come in a variety of configurations and sizes from small portable models to large-screen fixed models.

For computer users with low vision, there are a number of specialist software programmes which enable the user to access the screen by enlarging any selected section to the requisite size. Indeed some computers now have enlarge facility as standard. Such facilities bring most commercial software within the reach of the low vision user.

Enlargement

There is considerable controversy in the literature regarding the relative effectiveness of the use of large print and standard print with Low Vision Aids. There has been a tendency in educational circles to encourage children towards LVAs, regarding large print as at best a stepping stone for children who are required to read large amounts of material but have not yet mastered the techniques required to use LVAs. (Chapman and Stone 1979). Large print is criticised as being expensive and relatively difficult to provide and Corn (1980) suggested that the teacher who continuously provides large print copies rather than developing use of LVAs is 'discouraging the development of responsibility'.

Large print is not commonly used as the sole medium for study purposes in further and higher education because of the relative difficulty and expense of producing materials in large quantities for individuals. Although most libraries carry a selection of large print editions of book titles these are for leisure reading rather than study. However many partially sighted people with access to a photocopier with an enlarge facility find large print a comfortable medium for short documents. Standard commercial photocopiers found in many educational institutions have the facility to produce enlarged copies of either print text or diagrams with no significant loss of print quality, indeed in some cases the legibility of texts can be enhanced by producing a darker version of the original. One disadvantage of enlarging photocopiers is that enlarging text from A4 to A3 size produces large unwieldy documents. Scanning materials into computers using Optical Character Recognition (see below) allows text to be printed out on A4 in any chosen font size and the use of Laser or ink jet printers can provide very high quality print.

Adults with a visual impairment who use print for work or study usually adopt a combination of methods employing LVAs, CCTVs, personal readers or enlarged print depending on the nature of the task. Those with little or no useful residual vision can also access standard print directly through a variety of electronic reading devices

Enormous strides have been made in the development of speech synthesis for personal computers (Blenkhorn and Calderwood 1992) and it is widely used by blind people who use PCs for work or study. A recent concern has been the advent of the 'Windows' environment on PCs. Developed originally on the Apple Macintosh but now favoured in most computers in the workplace, Windows environments employ a 'Graphical User Interface' (GUI) system in which words are replaced with icons or symbols activated by use of a mouse. The icons cannot be translated by the current standard screen reading programs and this development has been seen as a further threat to the employment prospects of blind people.

Optical character recognition (OCR) offers a more direct access to print text. OCR machines allow the reader to place printed material onto a scanner (which resembles a photocopier in appearance). The page is electronically scanned and text is then reproduced in synthetic speech. OCR can be achieved through dedicated 'stand alone' reading machines which usually have a speech output or through systems designed to be installed on a standard personal computer where text can be stored in a word processing package and reproduced in hard copy via a braille embossing printer or large print.

Sullivan (1993) describes the results of bench tests on a variety of OCR systems and looks forward to cheap, easy, user-friendly models for the home user. Although Windows-based OCR systems will become more widely available it is uncertain how well blind users will be able to use this type of software given the essentially visual nature of GUI environments.

Current and future technological developments should enormously increase the potential for access to print by blind students. Compact disc (CD) technology promises to open up new avenues of access. CDs store enormous amounts of information and as books and reference materials become available on CD they can be downloaded via a PC to a printer or braille embosser to produce braille or large print texts or accessed immediately through screen enlargement or synthesised speech. Gill (1993) describes how the transmission of digital information into the home by teletext is only one of a variety of initiatives being considered by the European Community's Technology Initiative for Disabled and Elderly People (TIDE) programme to improve access to information for the visually impaired.

Print writing

Computers with synthesised speech, on-screen enlargement facilities and traditional mechanical or electronic typewriters offer touch typists with a visual impairment effective methods of producing print.

However for many students with a visual impairment handwriting remains the most important method of communication through the written word. A water-based black felt tip pen will produce a clearer script than a ballpoint pen and can be used with heavily lined matt paper available from the Partially Sighted Society. Most adventitiously blind people retain the ability to write and various templates are available to assist the handwriting of signatures on cheques or addresses and even letters. Some congenitally blind people may never have been taught how to write their own signature and this skill should form part of training programmes in life skills classes.

Taped materials

For many years taped materials have been available to the blind and increasingly information from national and local government is being produced in braille, large print and on tape. Audiotape may offer the student in further or higher education the only practical way of processing the large amounts of information coursework demands.

Substantial research into the potential of tape as a study medium for blind users was conducted in the 1960s and early '70s as tape recorders became readily available and affordable. Research centred on the use of variable speed tape recorders which allowed the user to process recorded material at two or three times normal conversational speed. Speech speeded to these levels inevitably raises the pitch of the speaker's voice producing an irritating 'Mickey Mouse' effect so specialist machines were developed which had additional controls to lower the pitch of the voice to normal, levels while maintaining the increased speed. 'Compressed speech', as this form of facility is known, allows the listener to maintain comprehension at speeds of over 275 words per minute (more than twice the speed of braille reading) giving people with visual impairments the ability to approach and even surpass silent reading rates achieved by sighted adults.

The advantages of tape over braille as a study medium include the increased speed of information processing it allows. Tapes are generally easier to prepare than braille texts and in the UK a number of charitable and commercial outlets offer quick turnaround preparation of taped materials on request e.g. the RNIB Express Reading Service.

Reading through touch

Of the estimated total population of nearly a million people with a visual impairment in the UK, 19,000 have learned braille well enough to be able to read a braille magazine or a book (Bruce et al. op. cit.). Of these 13,000 remain active readers while 10,000 write in braille. Given the high levels of association between visual impairment and braille one might be surprised to learn that braille apparently is such a little used medium. However if one considers only the 18,000 people registered blind in the 16-59 age range its importance becomes obvious. 81% of this group have been taught braille, and 51% learned braille well enough to be able to read. Approximately half of the 3000 registered blind who are in paid employment, use braille at work, so clearly for many of those with the severest visual disabilities, braille is an essential skill. There is little evidence that the demand for braille is in decline. The RNIB compared the results of its survey with those of an earlier survey taken in 1965 (Gray and Todd 1968) and found that there had been a proportional overall increase in braille readership among the registered blind in the 16-59 age group. While 33% of registered blind in 1965 had never learnt braille, by 1986 this figure had dropped to only 19%.

Reading through Braille

Reading through braille allows the advantages of working from hard copy. A competent braille reader is in complete control of the text can vary the pace of reading according to the complexity of the material. The braille reader can easily review and scan the text, or skip sections as required. In its contracted form (Grade 2) braille allows the average reader to achieve reading speeds of around 100-120 words per minute, considerably slower than the average sighted silent reading rate but nevertheless a satisfactory rate for many applications.

In the UK braille tuition is available through a variety of sources. In the 16-59 age group the major providers in the UK are welfare services (e.g. rehabilitation officers for the visually impaired) schools, colleges and specialist rehabilitation centres. Harley et al. (1979) commented that very little can be found in academic literature concerned with the specific area of teaching braille to the late blinded. The bulk of research has been centred upon the teaching of reading to children through braille. However, in many cases adults learning braille have previously been competent print readers and are coming to braille with different needs and training requirements.

Although there is no standard text on the theory and methodology of teaching braille to adults, there is general agreement in the literature that does tackle the subject that those teaching braille to adults need to be aware that reading readiness is just as important an element of successful teaching with adults as it is with children. Harley et al (op. cit.) defined readiness in terms of emotional readiness, perceptual readiness and academic readiness.

The loss of sight, whether it happens after a gradual deterioration or a sudden accident, inevitably requires a period of readjustment during which the person may undergo a process akin to grieving or mourning. Dodds et al (1992a,b) note that anxiety and depression are very prevalent in the early stages of adjustment to sight loss and raises the possibility that many clients need personal psychological rehabilitation before they can give of their best in any vocational assessment or training. The association between blindness and braille is strong and consciously or sub-consciously braille may come to be seen as confirmation of blindness and attempts to teach braille may be resisted on that basis.

Efficient braille reading requires fine tactile discrimination. It is generally accepted that initial training in tactile discrimination is necessary before a braille reading programme is embarked upon. The ability to make fine discriminations through touch may be impaired in some late beginners. Road accident victims who have lost their sight as a result of head injuries may also have associated neurological impairment affecting the sensitivity of their fingertips. People who lose their sight as a result of diabetic retinopathy often experience fluctuating touch sensitivity. Physical disabilities and conditions such as hemiplegia may allow people to use only one hand for reading and writing and will require specialised teaching approaches.

Another area where there is considerable consensus among practitioners who regularly teach braille to late beginners is on the need for academic readiness. The complexity of the braille code is well attested (Lorimer et al. 1982) and the memory load is substantial.

The decision to embark upon learning braille must ultimately be taken by the individual learning it. Without motivation and readiness learning is unlikely to succeed. For the late beginner who decides to embark upon braille a variety of teaching schemes are available. Although most of these schemes allow for independent study, access to an experienced braille tutor can make the learning process easier. Unless correct reading techniques are established from the outset, readers are unlikely to achieve sufficient fluency of reading to make braille an efficient reading medium. The braille reading schemes published by the RNIB are outlined briefly below:

'Beginning Braille' was written by Dr Michael Tobin of the Research Centre for the Education of the Visually Handicapped at the University of Birmingham. It comprises four braille booklets, four instructional audio cassettes and a print pamphlet and the course begins with enlarged 'Jumbo' braille. The materials are largely self instructional but can also be used in a teaching situation.

'Feeling Fine' written by Mark Pivac is a course which uses life skills as a basis for instruction and the braille reading matter contains elements such as sports results, shopping lists etc. This is in twelve units and the early units are presented in grade 1 and braille. It is accompanied by a commentary on six cassettes and a handbook in print and braille.

'Braille Made Easy – As Pye' was developed at the National Library by Leslie Pye to introduce adult readers to uncontracted Grade 1 braille. It consists of one volume in Jumbo braille and one accompanying cassette. A follow up version which introduces grade 2 braille has just been published.

'Fingerprints–a braille reading and writing course' is the latest addition to the field. Developed by Nigel Berry it is based upon materials developed in the course of his work as braille tutor for students at the Royal National College for the Blind in Hereford. It comprises eleven volumes and ten cassettes. At the early stages it contains advice on braille reading technique and offers pre-braille exercises to develop touch. It introduces both reading and writing, and while it allows for independent study, it is assumed that the learner will have some access to tutorial support. Fingerprints was designed for 16 to 25 year olds who have been competent print readers, although it has been successfully employed with older people in the course of its thorough development.

Although the National Library for the Blind do stock some books in Grade 1 braille, the majority of the reading material published in the UK is in Grade 2 braille, a heavily contracted code. To acquire mastery of Grade 2 braille learners have to be familiar with 126 rules and recognise by touch 189 different signs made up of combinations of dots. The same patterns of dots are used repeatedly in different orientations and the same signs may assume different meanings according to the context in which they appear.

Inevitably the learning of braille presents a considerable challenge and demands a high degree of motivation and perseverance from the beginner. Most braille reading schemes designed for adults assume that the learner already has a mastery of print reading and is seeking in braille an alternative medium of expression. But the visually-impaired young person or adult with additional learning difficulties may have only partly developed literacy and the tutor's responsibility is the teaching of reading in addition to the introduction of braille.

There is evidence to suggest that among the younger blind population the prevalence of additional learning disability is increasing. The RNIB report 'New Directions' published in 1990 suggests that there are in the region of 6000 multiply handicapped visually-impaired children aged from birth to nineteen in the UK, the majority of whom have moderate or severe learning difficulties. People with additional learning difficulties who receive support are to be found in a variety of education and welfare settings including specialist and non-specialist colleges of further education, and day and residential centres. Advice for people with visual impairments seeking basic educational help in mainstream adult education and for their tutors is available through the Basic Education and Skills Service (BESS) and details are available from the adult literacy co-ordinator at the RNIB Vocational Centre in Loughbrough. An adult literacy pack comprising six workbooks is available in print, tape and tactile modes from RNIB customer services. For people learning English as a second language *'When Paths Meet'* is a collection of simple stories about newcomers to the UK and could be useful in some adult literacy classes.

For a number of visually-impaired people with significant additional learning disabilities, Grade 2 braille is too complex a medium for communication. This does not imply that literacy is necessarily beyond the capabilities of these people but it does suggest that in Grade 2 braille they may well be presented with an unsuitable medium for learning. For some blind people with additional learning difficulties, even braille in its uncontracted Grade 1 form will prove too difficult. For those who lack the fine discrimination skills demanded by braille but are capable of literacy, an alternative code called Moon may be appropriate.

Moon

Moon is based on a simplified raised line version of the print alphabet and was invented in 1847 by Dr William Moon of Brighton.

Despite the world-wide dominance of braille, Moon has survived in the UK, perhaps because of its accessibility and simplicity when compared to braille. It has found a role amongst the elderly blind who are able to learn Moon with relative ease, partly because it bears some resemblance to the print which most of this population will have used throughout their lives. Moon is larger and bolder than braille and is much less contracted; as a result it takes up much more space than braille, and while its bulk makes Moon an inefficient medium for accomplished touch readers, it has been successfully used by some blind people with learning difficulties (McCall and Stone 1992).

Books and periodicals in Moon are published by the RNIB and the National Library for the Blind houses over 3000 books in Moon. The RNIB has produced a Moon teaching pack which it distributes free of charge.

Braille for sighted learners

For sighted adults who wish to learn the braille code, the RNIB Braille Primer has been the traditional learning medium. It was designed primarily as a teaching aid for transcribers of braille and hence doesn't allow the development of sight reading of braille.

The National Library for the Blind are in the process of publishing the Birmingham Braille Course which has been developed over several years for the use of teachers/lecturers of the visually impaired training at the University of Birmingham's School of Education. It comprises a workbook in print and braille, and is accompanied by a Rulebook which is a detailed reference guide to the rules of braille. Sighted learners requiring a qualification in braille can register for training with the RNIB National Education Centre which offers a distance taught training programme leading to a certificate in competency.

Writing tactile codes

About 25% of braillists still make use of the stylus and handframe which is a convenient and quiet way of taking notes but mechanical braille writing devices have been available for more than a century. In the UK the Perkins braille writer is by far the most favoured mechanical writer. The Perkins has six keys, each key corresponding to a dot in the braille cell. When pressed in the appropriate combination the keys reproduce on manilla paper braille letters and signs.

In recent years a variety of electronic braille writing devices have become available. These too are based around the six key format allowing braille input. Output may take the form of synthetic speech or a constantly renewable tactile display on the machine itself. The machines vary considerably in sophistication but range in price from a few hundred pounds to over £3000. Most electronic braille writing devices are 'paperless' allowing the user to store text in the machines own memory for subsequent transfer.

When hard copy is required most of these machines can be connected to peripherals such as standard printers or braille embossers. Some have built-in disc drives and store text onto discs or ram cards compatible with PCs. Most have sophisticated word processing capabilities and translation programmes which accept grade 1 or grade 2 braille. These machines have the advantage of being light and portable, some weighing sixteen ounces and most operating from mains or rechargeable batteries.

At present there is a debate on the question of dedicated braille writing devices. It is argued that touch typing using standard keyboards together with synthetic speech allows the blind to access standard technology developed for the sighted and that the teaching of typing should take priority over instruction in the use of specialist braille writers.

Voice activated computers which allow users to input text into PCs through speech are already available and while at this stage in their development they are expensive, it is intriguing to speculate that ultimately the spoken word may become the standard input system for sighted and blind users alike.

For many years Moon was not considered a true avenue to literacy because it was a reading medium only. The advent of the mechanical Moonwriter in 1986 and more recently the Moonframe, a simple device for writing Moon by hand, have improved the situation although the Moonwriter has not been the success that was anticipated and there is still a need for the development of a simple mechanical Moon embosser. It has now also become possible to reproduce good quality reading materials in Moon using a standard personal computer and swell paper, and Moon fonts are now available for a variety of computers.

Studying through braille

One of the difficulties that faces students using braille as a study medium in further and higher education is in acquiring specialist texts for coursework. For many purposes tape is a convenient substitute, but there is a wide selection of study material readily available in braille

The RNIB Braille Library has 60,000 braille copies, most of which are intended to support blind students in further and higher education and professional workers. Where the required text is 'not already available in braille, there are many organisations which offer transcription services on a voluntary and commercial basis. All the major national braille producers and local resource centres who offer transcription facilities can be found listed in *The In Touch Handbook* (Ford and Heshel, 1992) Organisations which offer electronic transcription can obviously turn around materials much quicker than those which offer only manual transcription. Transcription times can be speeded still further if the original text is supplied to the transcriber on disc.

Students in higher and further education and their tutors can receive advice on study methods including braille and tape, equipment, examination arrangements and library services from the Further and Higher Education Student Support Unit at the RNIB Vocational College in Loughborough. Advice is also available concerning entitlement to financial assistance for the purchase of specialist equipment, the payment of readers etc from the Disabled Students Allowance provided by LEAs to students receiving mandatory awards.

Conclusion

In this chapter it has only been possible to provide a brief overview of the issues and options concerning communication for young people and adults with visual impairments, but it is clear that resources and support are available to allow this section of the population access to the written word in the home, the college and the workplace. The ability to communicate successfully through the written word is central to academic and vocational success. On this basis anxieties must remain about the extent to which equal access has been achieved. Sighted people are four times more likely to be employed than blind people, and where the visually impaired do find employment it is proportionately more likely to be at an unskilled or semi skilled level rather than at professional or managerial level (Bruce et al. op. cit.). Significantly the evidence points to the fact that those who make use of special equipment and additional clerical

108

support such as personal readers are more likely to obtain and retain employment. The challenge surely now is to exploit the substantial developments in information technology and to continue to pursue entitlement to communication skills to enable the broad body of people with visual impairments to achieve equal opportunities for personal advancement.

References

Bruce I., McKennell.A. and Walker E. (1991) *Blind and Partially Sighted Adults in Britain: the RNIB Survey Volume 1* (London: HMSO).

Blenkhorn P. and Calderwood D. (1992) 'Access to Personal Computers Using Speech Synthesis', *New Beacon*, LXXVI,185-188.

Corn A.L., (1980) 'Optical Aids in the Classroom'. *Education of the Visually Handicapped.*

Chapman E.K.C. and Stone J.M. (1988) *The Visually Handicapped Child in Your Classroom* (London:Cassell).

Dodds A., Ng L., and Yates L. (1992a) 'Residential Rehabilitation. 1–Client Characteristics' *New Beacon*, LXXVI, 321-325.

Dodds A., Ng L., and Yates L. (1992b) 'Residential Rehabilitation. 2–Psychological outcome of rehabilitation', *New Beacon*, LXXVI, 373-377.

Ford M. and Heshel T.(1992) *The 1992-3 In Touch Handbook* (London: BBC Broadcasting Support Services).

Gray P., and Todd, J.E. (1968) *Mobility and reading habits of the blind* (London: HMSO).

Harley R.K., Henderson F.M. and Truan M.B. (1979) *The teaching of Braille Reading* (Illinois: Charles C. Thomas).

Lorimer J., Tobin M.J., Gill J., Douce J.L. (1982) *A Study of Braille Contractions,* (London: RNIB).

McCall S. and Stone J.M. (1992) 'Literacy for blind children through Moon- a possibility?' *British Journal of Visual Impairment,* 10(2), 53-54.

New Directions–towards a better future for multihandicapped visually impaired children and young people: Report of the Working Party on Services to Multihandicapped Visually Impaired Children and Young People. (1990) (London: RNIB)

Sullivan D., (1993) 'OCRs–Reading Technology Comes of Age', *New Beacon*, LXXVII, 145-150.

Useful additional reading

Simple Factsheets on various aspects of information technology for people with visual impairments, including large character displays, electronic reading and writing aids and tape recorders are available from the RNIB Employment Development and Technology Unit, 224 Great Portland Street, London W1N 6AA. These fact sheets offer descrpitions of equipment together with details of specification and suppliers

Harley R.H., Truan M.B. and Sandford L.D. (1987) *Communication Skills for Visually Impaired Learners* (Springfield, Illinois: Charles C. Thomas), is generally regarded as the standard text in this area, and although the emphasis is on the school based learner it is an invaluable resource.

Olson M., (19—) *Guidelines and Games for Teaching Efficient Braille Reading* (New York: AFB) is a short practical booklet designed for teachers of children but is an excellent introduction for the newcomer working with braille users at any level. Available through the RNIB National Education Centre.

CHAPTER TEN

Further Education and Training: A European Perspective

Terry Gould

This chapter examines the HELIOS (Handicapped People in the European Community Living Independently in an Open Society) project and its work in Britain. It also examines the philosophy and curriculum involved in rehabilitation for the visually impaired. Finally issues raised by the regionalisation of rehabilitation are addressed, along with possible strategies that might be adopted for future provision.

The Council of Europe, one of the oldest European institutions, fully supports the needs and rights of disabled persons in Europe. The council was established by ten nations on 5 May, 1949. The Committee for the Rehabilitation and Resettlement of the Disabled (Partial Agreement) is composed at present of experts from the Ministries of Labour, National Insurance and of Public Health of the following member States: Austria, Belgium, France, Germany, Italy, Luxembourg, Netherlands, Norway, Portugal, United Kingdom Spain and Switzerland .

In Resolution A.P (84) 3 (1) on a coherent policy for the Rehabilitation of Disabled People it states that 'more than 500 million people in the world are disabled as a consequence of physical, mental or sensory impairment'. It recognises that the rehabilitation of disabled people as a means of securing their integration in working life and society is the duty of the community and a guarantee of respect for human dignity and should be included in their priority objectives in social policy.

The first Community to come together was the European Coal and Steel Community (ECSC), in 1952, followed by the European Economic Community (EEC) in 1958 and the European Atomic Energy Community (Euratom) in 1958. The three communities' aims and objectives are serviced by: The European Parliament; The Council; The Commission and The Court of Justice.

Since 1967 there has been a single Commission and a single Council, which exercise all the powers and responsibilities vested in their respective predecessors by the three Community Treaties. The merger of the institutions was seen as the first step towards setting up a Single European community to be governed by a single treaty, replacing the Paris Treaty of 1958 which established the European Coal and Steel Community (ECSC) and the Rome Treaty 1958 which established the EEC and Euratom.

The Assembly has 518 Members of the European Parliament (MEPs). France, Germany, Italy and the UK each have 81, Spain 60, the Netherlands 25 Belgium, Greece and Portugal 24 each, Denmark sixteen, Ireland fifteen and Luxembourg five.

The Council is made up of representatives of the governments of the twelve member states. Each government sends one of its ministers. Its membership thus varies with the subjects down for discussion. The Foreign Minister is regarded as the country's main representative but other ministers also meet frequently for specialised council meetings and sometimes sit alongside the Foreign Ministers. The presidency of the Council rotates between the member governments at six monthly intervals.

When decisions are taken in the Council by majority vote, Germany, France, Italy and the United Kingdom have ten votes, Spain eight votes, Belgium, Greece, the Netherlands and Portugal five each, Denmark and Ireland three each and Luxembourg two votes. A qualified majority means 54 votes of the total of 76.

The Commission consists of seventeen members appointed by agreement between the member governments. They have a four year term of office and members must remain independent of the governments and of the Council. The Council cannot remove any member from office. Parliament, however, can pass a motion of censure compelling the Commission to resign as a body (in which case it would continue to handle everyday business until its replacement).

The Court of Justice is composed of thirteen judges appointed for six years by agreement among the governments, and ensures that implementation of the Treaties is in accordance with the rule of law.

The Council and Commission have the power to issue Regulations; Directives; Decisions and Recommendations and Opinions. Regulations are of general application and are binding in their entirety and applicable in all member states. Directives are binding on the Member States to which they are addressed as regards the results to be achieved, but leave the form and methods of achieving it to the discretion of national authorities. Decisions may be addressed to a government, an enterprise or a private individual; they are binding in their entirety on those to whom they are addressed. Recommendations and Opinions are not binding. There is however a discrepancy in terminology between the Paris and the two Rome Treaties which can be confusing. An ECSC recommendation is a binding enactment corresponding to the EEC and Euratom directive, whereas an EEC recommendation is not binding and is no stronger than an opinion.

HELIOS

Projects for inclusion in the HELIOS (Handicapped People in the European Community Living Independently in an Open Society) Programme were nominated by member states of the European Community and were selected by the Department of Health and the Employment Department, in association with other relevant Departments. Queen Alexandra College of Further Education for blind and partially-sighted students was selected as one of six rehabilitation centres to represent the interests of this country's blind and partially sighted people in an important European initiative aimed at improving the training of disabled people in the European Community (EC) – the Second Action Programme For The Disabled.

These six centres deal with all aspects of disability covered by HELIOS programme. To maximise the impact of the programme in the United Kingdom, Queen Alexandra College established an outer network of twelve members representing all aspects of the education and welfare of people with a visual disability. The goal of HELIOS was to disseminate information and to broaden the knowledge of members of advances in the education and training of disabled people throughout the European Community.

There are several factions in the UK that do not necessarily facilitate working together and quite often look as if they are pulling in opposite directions. The issues that appear to be polarising are:
1. Integration *v* segregation.
2. Organisations of the disabled *v* organisations for the disabled.

3. Organisations that want change *v* organisations that want to maintain the status quo.
4. Centralisation *v* subsidiarity.
5. A combination of all the above issues and the inter-relationship between them.

The best work that has emerged from HELIOS is the networks that have developed, facilitated initially by Brussels and the HELIOS programme. These networks and transitional projects are undertaking practical research into everyday problems and are less concerned with semantics and political manoeuvring.

Partnerships are important and results emerge if there are dynamic groupings where decisions can be made quickly and practical solutions implemented on the basic of good practical applications of research which are then extended to transitional partners.

Many traditional institutions for the blind have so many bureaucratic blocking mechanisms and communities so large that progress is slow and tedious. The outside world is changing so rapidly that long protracted research and fine words are no longer sufficient to meet the real needs of blind people.

Networking requires new thinking, lateral unity and new alliances. Direct provision and direct action with people and organisations who have the will to initiate meaningful strategies to improve conditions for blind people are essential. What is reprehensible is the emergence of empire building groups using current philosophies that may well be detrimental to blind people but who are prepared to risk new ventures because what has happened in the past has been so slow, so predictable and so traditional.

For blind and partially sighted people in the United Kingdom, networking has been one of the most successful and productive aspects of the HELIOS programme. Queen Alexandra College initiated an Outer Network within the UK to inform other training organisations of what was happening in the HELIOS programme and to co-ordinate any comments that Outer Network members wished to raise at plenary sessions or thematic seminars. The UK Outer Network for Rehabilitation Centres For the Blind was based on geographical criteria and organisation criteria. The UK Outer Network created by Queen Alexandra College was composed of ten different organisations and thirteen different institutions. Eight of the representatives were invited to participate in study trips in Europe. Those who actually took up the invitation were Peter Talbot of the

Royal London Society For the Blind, Mike Rowe of the Royal National Institute For the Blind, John Collins of Partially Sighted Society and Alan Suttie of Fife Society for the Blind.

It was after one of these study visits that the concept of working together and closer networking within the UK began to take shape. Peter Talbot and Terry Gould began tentative steps to work seriously together. Although an ad hoc grouping with most of the ten organisations sharing ideas had been in existence for several years, there was never an open sharing. Quite often larger organisations for the blind never fully participated. There was a decided lack of trust in all parties concerned. Several training institutions met together under another umbrella called the Heads of Independent Schools and Colleges Group. Within this group there was superficial working together but again there was an underlying atmosphere of lack of trust and vested interest. This small mindedness was not, and is not, in the best interests of blind and partially-sighted people. It was to this end that the Royal London Society for the Blind and Birmingham Royal Institution for the Blind, through their two principal officers Peter Talbot and Terry Gould, began to work together on a joint project that would benefit blind people directly. Julia Schofield's company was commissioned to research a pilot project using multi-media technology to enable blind and partially-sighted people to access learning and training packages. The pilot study looked promising and a joint European project was explored, bringing in European partners. This European project had potential not only for blind and partially-sighted people but for other disability groups and also for training packages for mainstream colleges and commercial companies. At last the parochialism of organisations for the blind was being called into question – but in a positive way to produce interactive and open learning materials for all people. The packages for blind and partially-sighted people of course need tailoring for the specific disability, as, maybe, will some of the other packages. More European partners have now expressed interest in the project HELIOS has been directly responsible for the outcomes so far achieved.

Queen Alexandra College in Birmingham is a college of further education that offers blind and partially sighted students a range of pre-vocational and vocational courses not necessarily linked to traditional 'blind' occupations. Its primary aim is to provide further education and training to enable blind and partially-sighted students to realise their personal, social and vocational potential. Of the current 140 students, half are registered blind and half are partially sighted. There are three types of vocational preparation courses. The Foundation Course provides basic training in braille and basic living skills. A second course leads to the Diploma in Vocational Education, allowing students to sample a range of vocational courses to enable them to choose one they wish to pursue at vocational level. The subjects include engineering, typing, word processing, information processing, child care, catering, upholstery, cycle mechanics, music production, craft and design, glass engraving, production assembly training and retail and business studies. The college has a philosophy of meeting individual needs and currently 24 students are studying full-time in mainstream colleges and 25 are in modular courses, also in mainstream colleges.

HELIOS was established by the Council of Europe in 1988, as part of the Second Community Action Programme for Disabled People. UK involvement in the First Action Programme was essentially through the participation of three employment rehabilitation centres and two district projects, together with a national steering group. A report by a House of Lords Select Committee in 1988 was very critical concerning the nature and outcome of the UK part of the First Action Programme. In particular, a higher level of co-ordination and supervision at national level, more publicity and greater involvement of voluntary organisations were recommended for UK involvement in the Second Programme.

In implementing the HELIOS programme the Commission is assisted by two formal consultative bodies: the Advisory Committee with two government representatives from each member state, and the Liaison Group in which these same officials are joined by nine representatives of the selected non-governmental organisations in the disability field. Among other significant bodies in the context of HELIOS is the Dialogue Groups whose membership is drawn from 31 selected European or international non-governmental organisations (NGOs) and includes the nine non-government members of the Liaison Group. A number of projects were critical of the fact that the views and interests of people with disabilities had only featured in the overall organisation of the HELIOS Programme via especially representatives of European organisations in the Liaison Group and the NGO Dialogue Group. The activities of HELIOS are managed by a specially appointed Team of Experts who have constituted the participating projects' main points of contact with the EC.

Project co-ordinators spoke very positively about the help and advice they had received from the expert with responsibility for their particular network. These 'front experts' were widely seen as both approachable and supportive.

In the United Kingdom HELIOS has two parts: the EC network of rehabilitation centres and the EC network of local model projects which is split into three areas:

1. School integration.
2. Economic integration, locations training and employment.
3. Social integration (mobility and transport, accessibility, and co-ordination of housing).

An important characteristic is the interaction among these parts since an aim of HELIOS is to increase technical co-operation and to improve the co-ordination of different activities at community level. To achieve a community approach in all areas requires the wide exchange of professional knowledge about innovations and experiments. The means to attain the objectives of HELIOS can be summed up in the following key words: interaction, information, co-ordination, innovation, exchange and transfer.

The information and document service edited the HELIOS magazine which provided a major forum for the exchange and dissemination of information throughout Europe. First published in 1988 the magazine was available three times a year in nine Community languages and had a circulation of 45,000 throughout Europe The documentation centre holds a comprehensive stock of official EC documents and texts.

Mixed-provision (the development of individual learning programmes) has long been in existence at Queen Alexandra College. For integration to be successful, however, the student needs to have the tools and sufficient support in the integrated setting. As training at Queen Alexandra College matches this flexible client-centred approach to the needs of the student and how best they can be met, this philosophy seems more sensible than outright adoption of a policy of integration for its own sake. A balanced philosophy and flexible thinking by trained staff with a European perspective should enhance the prospects of all disabled people in the 1990s if adequate resources are available.

The Council of Ministers is debating the next action programme for disabled people. Recommendations as a result of the HELIOS programme have been made at the plenary conferences to get more 'action' and less talking. This is something that Queen Alexandra College has actively encouraged. As Principal of Queen Alexandra College with other colleagues, I have had an opportunity to see what Europe has to offer. Likewise visitors have been able to visit Queen Alexandra College and see what we have to offer. Queen Alexandra College has been referred to as one of the most advanced colleges in Europe, offering a wide range of opportunities to blind and partially sighted people that are not available in most mainland European countries. Hopefully we have influenced thinking regarding future developments in Europe and HELIOS 2 will act as the catalyst for future dissemination and exchange of ideas.

HELIOS 2

On 2 October 1991 the Commission adopted the proposal for a Council decision establishing the Third Community Action Programme For Disabled People, HELIOS 2 1992-1996. It has not happened yet but it could happen. What the Commission seeks to achieve through HELIOS 2 is to strengthen the economic and social cohesion of the people of Europe and to re-state its firm resolve to continued and intensive work on a global coherent policy for the integration of disabled people. HELIOS 2 continues the successful work undertaken under HELIOS 1, and extends its scope to new fields with work being reconstructed to benefit from past experience. HELIOS 2 will cover such new areas as prevention and early assistance, functional rehabilitation, integration in nursery schools and higher education, continuing training and access to creative activities, sport and tourism. The new technologies and especially their integration and potential will be given a more prominent place in all fields of activity. Examples include work place adaptation and mobility independence, living in the home environment, counteracting the isolation of disabled people, and as educational and vocational training tools. Public awareness raising and the provision of information on disability issues will be a priority. The advisory role of non-governmental organisations will be strengthened to enable more benefit to be gained from the experience and from the dynamic effect of innovative measures.

   Technical co-operation within the European networks with existing activities in the member states will be pursued in a differently structured form according to more precisely formulated methods and measures. Four subject fields are affected here functional rehabilitation, educational, economic and social interaction and independent living.

The Handinet system, which is designed to provide information on all essential matters concerning the specific needs of disabled people, became operational in 1990. It comprises a database plus electronic mail and journal facilities. At the end of 1991 the first Handinet system module relating to technical aids and known as Handiaids came into effect. Using a compact disc, CD-ROM information can be obtained on more than 10,000 technical aid products by reference to function, technical detail and price (in ECU).

HELIOS 2 was born after very extensive consultations involving all interested parties. It is funded to the tune of 46.3 million ECU for a period of five years, 1992-1996. The new five year HELIOS 2 programme is concerned with all categories of disabled people and aims to continue to promote and intensify the kind of activities undertaken under HELIOS 1, stimulating work of a model nature in the member states. It also seeks to foster the co-operation and co-ordination of measures at local, regional, national and community levels with a view to finding convergent solutions at European level.

As a result of the 1988 Lords Select Committee, a refreshing development from the inception of HELIOS 1 was the Government Departments' interest and participation. The Department of Health and the Employment Department have played key roles in helping to disseminate information and bring together the various UK elements of the HELIOS programme. The forum for dissemination and exchange has been facilitated by plenary conferences and meetings held at various UK centres. The UK HELIOS team has been in the main well supported and well co-ordinated. Additional money should of course encourage even better co-ordination and better support.

As a centre selected by the UK Government departments, Queen Alexandra College has met the criteria that were set. The main thrust of the network of rehabilitation centres was for professionals in the dissemination and exchange of ideas and good practice. This dissemination of views was in the context of direct integration and ultimate integration.

Since 1988 the college has maintained continuing links with European countries. Such contacts have been made in a variety of ways which have included training sessions, study tours and plenary conferences. Besides the Principal, fourteen members of staff, including members of the Outer Network, have visited establishments in Italy, Denmark, Belgium, France, Germany, Greece, Ireland, Spain and the Netherlands. The College has been pleased to welcome visitors from Europe and other parts of the world.

In 1989 two blind professionals from Greece paid an extended visit to Queen Alexandra College to study teaching and training methods. The following year the college played host to the main European Seminar on Vocational Training For Blind And Partially Sighted People when ten countries and 27 delegates were present. In 1991 political changes in Eastern Europe were followed by the first Plenary Conference in what was East Germany. Along with other establishments Queen Alexandra College has shown itself ready to offer interest and support to the emerging democracies. Visitors to the College from other countries, including India, the Republic of China and Japan, have expressed great interest in the HELIOS project and have seen in it a blueprint for the positive change of social and political attitudes towards those with disabilities.

Within HELIOS there was no money for any projects other than study visits or training sessions. The students at Queen Alexandra College are not directly affected by that programme. However, the increased knowledge obtained by staff and the widening of training to encompass a European perspective will, it is hoped, lead to benefits for students. What is being learned is being assimilated into Queen Alexandra College, and contributing not only to a better informed staff but to better informed government departments, and better training opportunities for disabled people.

References

The Council of Europe Resolution AP (84) 3 'A coherent policy for the Rehabilitation of Disabled People' adopted by the Committee of Ministers on 17 September 1984 at the 375 meeting of the Ministers Deputies.

Emile Noel (1988) *Working Together: The Institutions of the European Community* (Luxembourg: The Office for Official Publications of the European Communities).

One Parliament For Twelve (1991), Euro Parliament U.K. Office, Queen Anne's Gate, London SW1 9AA. Telephone 071 222 0411.

Index

Act 2, 6, 6-16, 55
Further Education 38-40, 50, 53,
   89, 94, 96, 104
further education provision 85

GNVQs 30
governors 35
GUI 98-99

Handiaids 118
Handinet system 118
HELIOS 110-119
HELIOS magazine 116
HMI 30-31, 33, 36

independence 49, 89, 91
Industry Lead Bodies 36, 66-67
Information Technology 39, 46,
   57, 60-62
integration 38, 41, 50, 112, 117

LEAs 6-16, 30-31, 33, 36-37, 107
link courses 36-37
LVAs, 97-98

Magnification 96-97
Moon 47, 96, 104-106
multi-dimensional perspective 74
multi-media technology 114

National Council for Vocational
   Qualifications 30, 36, 65-66, 68
National Vocational
   Qualifications 3, 36, 53, 66, 69,
   72
needs analysis 56
Networking 113
non-governmental organisations
   (NGOs) 115, 117
norm referenced testing 79, 83

OCR 98, 99
open learning materials 114
over-protectiveness 87

PAC Team (PACTS) 25-26, 58-59

parents 50
PC 98-99, 106
performance criteria 67, 69, 71
piano tuning 60
PICKUP 53-64
pre-NVQ 36
pre-vocational and vocational
   courses 114
prior learning 36, 38

Quality assurance 65
Queen Alexandra College
   112-113, 116-119

Records of Achievement 38
rehabilitation 17-28, 46, 55, 58,
   96, 110, 112, 117-118
resources 42, 67
RNIB (Royal National Institute
   for the Blind) 7, 10-11, 14,
   23-24, 26, 39, 51, 54, 58,
   60-62, 72, 101-105, 107, 109,
   114
Royal London Society for the
   Blind 114
Royal National College 55-56,
   61, 63

Self assessment system 76, 83
self-concept 86-88, 90
self-esteem 88, 91
self-image 87, 90
self-worth 87-88, 91-92
SKILL 6-7, 37, 39, 51
social rehabilitation 19, 22
Social Services 31, 42, 44
Special Needs Co-ordinator 37,
   45
specialist colleges 37, 53, 55, 58
staff development 67
strategies 35, 67
support 39, 41-52
synthetic speech 96, 99, 106

TIDE 99
training 47-49, 55-60, 72-73